GREAT WALKS

DARTMOOR & EXMOOR

GREAT WALKS

DARTMOOR & EXMOOR

JOHN WEIR & BRIAN LE MESSURIER

Photography by John Heseltine

Series Editor Frank Duerden

© John W. H. Weir & Brian Le Messurier 1988
© Illustrations Ward Lock Limited

This special edition has been
produced in 1992
by New Orchard Editions Ltd,
Villiers House, 41/47 Strand,
London WC2N 5JE,
a Cassell company
for publication
by Printwise Publications Ltd,
47 Bradshaw Road, Tottington,
Bury, Lancs BL8 3PW

Photography by John Heseltine

Map artwork by Elly King

Printed and bound in Spain by Graficromo S. A.

ISBN 1-87222635-3

Half title page: *The foreshore at Porlock Bay,
with Porlock Weir in the background.*

Title page: *Crazywell Pool, south-west
Dartmoor, sits in an old mine working.*

CONTENTS

ACKNOWLEDGMENTS

Particular thanks go to the Dartmoor National Park Authority and the West Country Studies Library (Exeter), but the preparation of this book has been made possible with the help of many people. I also owe gratitude to others whose research of and care for Dartmoor has provided much inspiration and guidance.

John Weir

I am grateful to the following for assistance in the preparation of the Exmoor section: Mr Brian Miller; Mr Brian Pearce; Mr G.A. Osborn (Humberts).

Brian Le Messurier

INTRODUCTION

Of the ten National Parks in England and Wales only two—Dartmoor and Exmoor—are situated in the southern part of England. Dartmoor National Park lies wholly within the county of Devon between Exeter to the east and Plymouth to the west. Twenty-five miles (40 km) to the north north east, straddling Devon and Somerset and visible from Dartmoor, lies Exmoor National Park. Together they extend for some 630 sq miles (1631 sq km). Both areas have unique qualities and an essential integrity which makes them distinctively Dartmoor and Exmoor.

Dartmoor is the largest and wildest open space in southern England. The core of the National Park is an upland of granite rising to 2038 ft (621 m) at High Willhays. Two vast blocks of moorland in the north and the south are separated by the River Dart and its tributaries. Surrounding this moorland is Dartmoor's 'in-country'—an intimate enclosed landscape containing islands of common land. The moorland is characterized by wide expanses of bog and smooth contoured hills often crowned by rugged tors; here is the greatest density of prehistoric remains in north-western Europe. Mist and cloud frequently shroud the hills and the average rainfall is high. Streams and rivers rise in bogs and their valleys are wide in the upper reaches; where they leave the moor they cascade down waterfalls and run through rocky gorges in steep, wooded valleys.

Exmoor contains a wide variety of landscapes despite its comparatively small size. Unlike other south-west moorlands, Exmoor does not comprise granite; Devonian sedimentary rocks dominate most of the geology. The central plateau comprises sweeping moorland and to the north the land meets the sea abruptly in towering cliffs above the Bristol Channel. Here rocky headlands, steep wooded ravines and waterfalls combine to make this an area of exceptional beauty. The Exmoor panorama is also enhanced by deep wooded valleys and beech-hedged pasture. Dunkery Beacon, the highest point on Exmoor, rises to 1704 ft (520 m).

The beginnings of any landscape are in its rocks and the earth processes which act upon them, but a human occupation spanning over 6000 years in these uplands has left, and continues to leave, its mark; for Dartmoor and Exmoor this contribution has in the main added to endemic grandeur, beauty and interest—the result a rich natural and cultural heritage. Evidence abounds of past settlement and past industrial activity such as peat cutting, mining and quarrying. Hill farming dominates the scene and more modern incursions including forestry, reservoirs, larger scale quarrying, agricultural improvement and, on Dartmoor, military training, bring the landscape palimpsest to date.

Public access in both National Parks has been much improved in recent years. Within the two Parks over 1200 miles (1931 km) of paths—public rights of way and permitted paths—exist. Exmoor, like Dartmoor, has extensive tracts of moorland which extend walking possibilities; on Dartmoor, since 1985 following the Dartmoor Commons Act, there is a legal right of access to the 90,000 acres (36,423 ha) registered as common land. Both the National Park Authorities have undertaken virtually complete waymarking of the path networks within their responsibility and maintenance and improvements are on-going tasks. The information given within the walk route descriptions in this book, as far as is known, was accurate when collected. However, legal diversions and possible future access agreements may result in necessary deviations in the routes on one or two stretches—always use up to date maps where possible.

With an Ordnance Survey Landranger or Outdoor Leisure Map in hand it is virtually impossible for the walker not to encounter something of interest with every mile walked on these hills. In this sense, and given the extensive walking opportunities possible, the selection of walks has been a difficult task for both authors. These walks, however, do give a good geographical spread for both National Parks. But, do not look for all of the recognized great walks on Dartmoor in this book, such as the Lich Way—they have been adequately dealt with elsewhere; great walks are not so much determined by their length or historical origins but more by the way they are trod.

THE NATIONAL PARKS OF DARTMOOR & EXMOOR

In 1945 John Dower defined a National Park, in application to Great Britain, as 'an extensive area of beautiful and relatively wild country in which, for the nation's benefit and by appropriate national decision and action, (a) the characteristic landscape beauty is strictly preserved, (b) access and facilities for public open air enjoyment are amply provided, (c) wildlife and buildings and places of architectural and historic interest are suitably protected, while (d) established farming use is effectively maintained.'

The United Kingdom lagged behind many other countries of the world in establishing National Parks. The United States, Canada, Germany, Italy, New Zealand, South Africa, Spain, Switzerland and Sweden were among the countries which had National Parks before any were designated here.

Under the National Parks and Access to the Countryside Act of 1949 a National Parks Commission was established which was responsible for the creation of National Parks; ten were created by the Commission in England and Wales between 1950 and 1957—the Peak District, the Lake District, Snowdonia, Dartmoor, the Brecon Beacons, Exmoor, Northumberland, the Yorkshire Dales, North York Moors and Pembrokeshire Coast. In 1968 the National Parks Commission was replaced by the Countryside Commission which took over the responsibility for the Parks and which has responsibilities for the countryside as a whole. A further change came under the Local Government Act of 1972; under this Act a separate National Park Authority was set up in 1974 for all of the National Parks, with the exception of the Peak District and the Lake District; the latter two had similar status from their outset. All National Park Authorities were given the task of producing a National Park Plan by April 1977, and of reviewing that plan at intervals of not more than five years. These plans, and their reviews, set out the policies of each Authority for the management of its Park and proposals for carrying out those policies.

The Dartmoor and Exmoor National Park Authorities' responsibilities are geared to the twin purposes of National Parks—the conservation and enhancement of the quality of the landscape and the promotion of the enjoyment of that landscape by the public. These purposes must be pursued with the social and economic well-being of each National Park's community as an object of policy.

The responsibility of achieving these aims on Dartmoor lies with the Dartmoor National Park Committee, a Committee of Devon County Council. This has twenty-one members all of whom are appointed—eleven by the County Council, seven by the Secretary of State for the Environment and one by each of the three District Councils which overlap the Park almost entirely. The National Park Authority employs some fifty full time staff whose work involves planning; the conservation of landscape, wildlife, buildings and archaeological features; the management of informal recreation; the provision of information; and the administration of appropriate countryside legislation. To help achieve its purposes the Authority works closely with District and Parish Councils, amenity bodies, farmers and other individuals, and jointly with other public authorities.

The day-to-day work of the Dartmoor National Park Authority is funded almost 85 per cent by the taxpayer, directly from the Department of the Environment and, indirectly, through the Rate Support Grant to Devon County Council. The balance is met by the Devon ratepayer. The Authority also receives some income from the sale of publications and from certain services, such as fees payable for planning applications. During 1986–1987 the Dartmoor National Park Authority's budget was £1.25 million.

For Exmoor the 1986–87 budget was about £870,000, of which 75 per cent came directly from the Department of the Environment and 25 per cent from the Somerset and Devon County Councils.

Responsibility for Exmoor lies with the Exmoor National Park Committee, which also has twenty-one members—eight from Somerset County Council, four from Devon County Council and one each from the North Devon and West Somerset District Councils. The remaining seven members are appointed by the Secretary of State for the Environment. The Authority employs about thirty full-time staff, with ten estate workers. Further staff, working on a part-time basis, are employed by both Authorities in the summer.

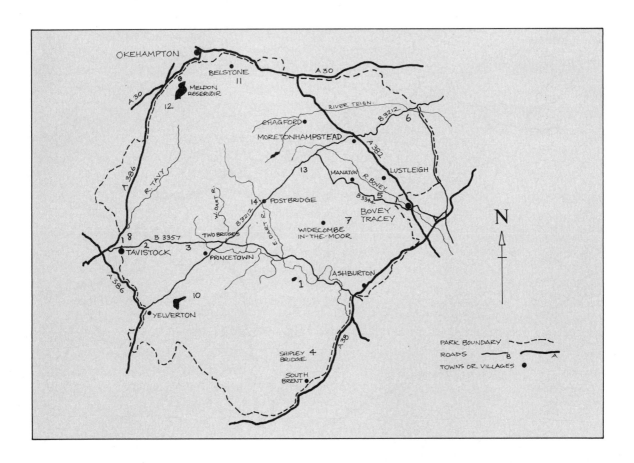

FIGURE 1 *The Dartmoor National Park. The numbers indicate the approximate starting points for the routes described.*

SOME FACTS AND FIGURES ABOUT THE DARTMOOR NATIONAL PARK

DESIGNATED	30 October 1951.
AREA	365 sq miles (945 sq km). It is the third smallest of the ten National Parks but represents the largest area of open space in England south of the Peak District.

LAND CONTROL IN 1987 (%)		
	Ministry of Defence (freehold, lease and licence)	14
	South West Water	3.8
	National Trust	3.8
	Forestry Commission (freehold or leasehold)	1.8
	Dartmoor National Park Authority	1.4

The rest of the land is in private ownership, including some 30% by the Duchy of Cornwall. 18% of the Park has been designated by the Nature Conservancy Council as Sites of Special Scientific Interest.

RESIDENTS	On the basis of the Census data the resident population of the National Park in 1981 was estimated as 29,139.
VISITORS	Approximately 7.75 million visitor days are made to the Park per annum; a large proportion of visitors are Devon residents.

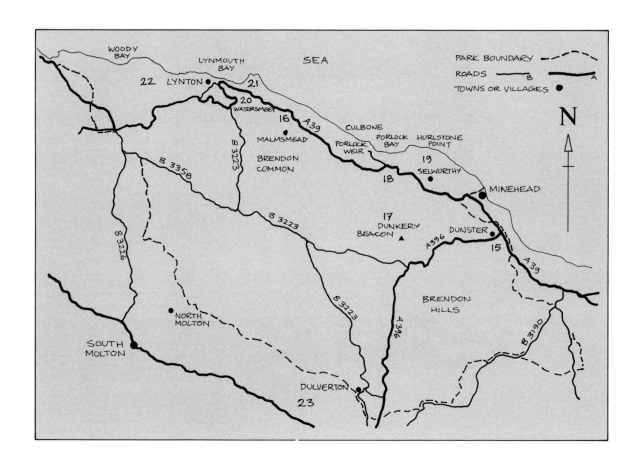

FIGURE 2 *The Exmoor National Park. The numbers indicate the approximate starting points for the routes described.*

SOME FACTS AND FIGURES ABOUT THE EXMOOR NATIONAL PARK

DESIGNATED	27 January 1954.
AREA	265 sq miles (686 sq km). Of the ten National Parks only the Pembrokeshire Coast National Park is smaller. 71% of Exmoor lies in Somerset and 29% in Devon.
LAND CONTROL IN 1987 (%)	79.1% of the total area of the Park is privately owned. The remaining 20.9% is owned by:

National Trust	10
National Park Authority	4.3
Crown Estate	3.5
Forestry Commission	2.0
South West Water	0.6
Ministry of Agriculture, Fisheries and Food	0.3
Town and District Councils	0.2

RESIDENTS	On the basis of the Census data the resident population of the Exmoor National Park was 9994 in 1981.
VISITORS	Approximately 2.8 million visitor days are spent in the Park each year.

THE FACE OF DARTMOOR

GRANITE AND TORS

Some 241 square miles (625 sq km)—66 per cent—of Dartmoor comprises one rock type—granite—which occurs in a single block with the exception of two small outcrops south of Lee Moor. The granite forms an elevated region, the topographical eminence of which dominates the Devon scene, and comprises wide sweeping moorland dotted with numerous bare rocky outcrops known as tors. This land rises to 2038 ft (621 m) above sea level at the small outcrop of High Willhays.

From the Devonian to the late Carboniferous periods (395–280 million years ago [Ma]) Dartmoor was part of a huge sea floor. Sediments were being deposited on it mainly by rivers flowing from mountains to the north. These sediments are now represented around the granite mass by slates, shales, mudstones, sandstones, limestones, cherts and conglomerates. During the late Carboniferous period these sediments were subject to intense pressure from the north and south—the result of a major tectonic episode, the Variscan Orogeny —causing their crumpling to form part of a folded mountain chain known as the Cornubian Mountains. Into the roots of these mountains, some 290–309 Ma, magma welled up and cooled to form granite. This granite occurs in south west England from the Scilly Isles to Dartmoor in a series of 'bosses', which are all linked within the earth's crust to form a batholithic complex which at 404 miles (650 km) in length is probably the largest in the world. The Cornubian Mountains were eroded away during the following Permian and Triassic periods and Dartmoor was again submerged under a shallow sea and a thin layer of chalk was deposited on it during the Cretaceous period (110–65 Ma). By the beginning of the Tertiary period (around 65 Ma) this chalk had been eroded away and earth movements which then followed in the late Cretaceous and mid-Tertiary periods gave Dartmoor its present day outline as new river courses and the agents of weathering attacked the granite.

There are several different types of granite, each of which is affected differently by weathering and erosion, and most tors comprise coarse granite. Tors owe their particular shapes to the pattern of cracks, or joints, which they all exhibit. Near vertical, or master, joints formed as the granite originally cooled and contracted; others formed as that cooling penetrated further inwards and yet more—so-called sheet joints—as the load of sedimentary rock above was eroded away so that, relieved of the weight, the granite sprang apart; finally as the granite itself was eroded so more cracks developed.

Much that is human in the Dartmoor landscape is of granite — prehistoric, late Saxon, medieval and modern houses; prehistoric stone circles, standing stones, stone rows and graves; barns, field boundaries, boundary stones, gateposts, troughs, querns and millstones; churches, chapels and crosses, bridges, paving kerbs, tramway rails and dams. And many of the tors themselves—such as Hound Tor, Vixen Tor and Devil's Tor—have become firmly embedded in Dartmoor folklore and legend. Almost everything that was built was indigenous and the present and the future should safeguard such an inheritance that has for so long survived.

BOGS AND MIRES

Bogs and mires on Dartmoor are the inevitable consequence of high altitude and rainfall and a largely impervious granite substrata.

Blanket bog, colloquially referred to as 'fen', occurs above the 1500 ft (457 m) contour and two large areas of it extend over 50 square miles (129 sq km) covering much of the northern and southern plateaux. It is composed of a thick layer of peat which has been laid down for hundreds of years. On the high north and south plateaux golden plover and dunlin breed—the most southerly breeding populations in the world.

Mires, or valley bogs, are scattered at the heads and along the courses of rivers and streams draining the high moors. They are characterized by bright green flush areas and their quaking surfaces known as 'featherbeds'. These bogs have also accumulated peat down the centuries by virtue of their position in valley bottoms or at a significant break of slope. Examples include Taw Marsh, Blackslade Mire and the notorious Foxtor Mires.

THE PREHISTORIC PAST

One of the finest prehistoric landscapes in western Europe can be found within the Dartmoor National Park. The most important remains date from the Bronze Age, which lasted from 2500 BC until about 500 BC.

The earliest remains, though limited in number, are Neolithic barrows; these are chambered tombs standing either as massive stones, which were used in the construction of the burial chamber itself, or as long low mounds. These tombs may well be 5000–6000 years old. From about 2000–1000 BC more barrows —the round barrows—were constructed. Many burials were in cists (kistvaens)—these consist of granite slabs forming a small box-like structure, many of which are now exposed to the elements.

About seventy prehistoric stone rows are known on Dartmoor. They are either single, double or triple rows and run roughly in a straight line. Their length varies—one, in the Erme Valley, is 2.1 miles (3.4 km) in length and is probably the longest stone row in the world. Some thirty-three free-standing stone

The Nine Maidens prehistoric retaining circle, flanked by Belstone Tor.

A new life begins.

circles exist whilst also present are tall upright stones (menhirs)—some over 10 ft (3 m) high—and stand either in isolation or are associated with stone rows. These enigmatic ritual monuments date from about 3000–1000 BC.

On Dartmoor survive the foundations of prehistoric homes which are known as hut circles and number over two thousand. They consist of a rough circle, 3.2–10.9 yds (3–10 m) in diameter, of closely-fitting stones forming a low wall with a gap for an entrance. The hut circles represent a span of at least two thousand years of settlement from about 2000 BC.

The least obvious relics of the Bronze Age, dating to about 3000 years old, are the land boundaries now known as reaves—the largest surviving Bronze Age field system in Europe. These low walls, appearing as banks, run straight and parallel to each other for up to several kilometres and are met at right angles by other reaves.

Fortified prehistoric settlements on Dartmoor are rare, but a few hillforts with substantial earth or stone ramparts can be found round the edges of the moor. These belong to the late prehistoric period, roughly 1000 BC–AD 50.

THE DARTMOOR COMMONS

Some 40 per cent of the Dartmoor National Park is common land—90,000 acres (36,423 ha), the bulk of it in a single block. It comprises the Forest of Dartmoor, the Commons of Devon —which abut the Forest boundary—and a scatter of manorial commons, some of them separated from the main block. This expanse of open space, the largest in England south of the Pennines, is the heart of Dartmoor's natural beauty and was one of the main reasons for Dartmoor being designated a National Park.

Like common land everywhere it has owners who own the freehold subject to the rights of others—the commoners. The origin of common land stretches back to time immemorial, older than the manors within whose regulation and control much of it subsequently fell. Whatever its history or origins, all common land and the rights to it are now registered under the Commons Registration Act, 1965.

A right of common is the right for commoners to take some part of the natural produce of the soil from land belonging to someone else. These rights have become attached to certain properties within the local community. Such rights practised include: the common of pasture—the right to graze animals; turbary—the right to take peat or turf for domestic use as fuel;

and, common in soil—the right to take timber and underwood. In each case, these rights are limited to the requirements of the commoner's land or house. The owner has the mineral and sporting rights and is entitled to the 'surplus' of this natural produce when the commoners' needs are satisfied. Historically the common of pasture is the most important of these rights and today ponies, cattle and sheep are the main interest.

There are legally 93 separate common land units on Dartmoor, with some 60 owners and over 1500 individual commoners. The Dartmoor Commons Act, 1985, promoted jointly by the Dartmoor National Park Authority and the Dartmoor Commoners' Association, is unique in that it addresses itself to the problem of management of the commons as well as the question of public access.

THE MINISTRY OF DEFENCE ON DARTMOOR

The Ministry of Defence (MoD) has control, either as owner or the holder of a lease or licence, of over 33,000 acres (13,300 ha) of the National Park. This training area contains three firing ranges (Okehampton, Merrivale and Willsworthy) the boundaries of which are marked on the ground by a series of red and white posts, and by noticeboards on the main approaches. All three ranges are on north Dartmoor and when wishing to walk there firing times will need to be checked. **Walks in this book which enter the Ranges are 2.8: Merrivale; 2.9: Okehampton; 3.11: Okehampton; 3.12: Okehampton and Willsworthy and 4.14: Okehampton and Merrivale.**

No firing takes place on Dartmoor on public holidays, nor during the month of August. Firing at other times is advertised in local newspapers every Friday and notices are displayed in neighbouring police stations, some post offices, some public houses and National Park Information Centres (open Easter to end of October), or you can use the telephone answering service on the following numbers: Torquay (0803) 24592; Exeter (0392) 70164; Plymouth (0752) 701924; Okehampton (0837) 2939.

When firing is in progress warning signals are displayed (red flags by day and red lights by night) on tor and hill summits in or abutting the ranges. Entry in the range(s) during such times is forbidden and, of course, unsafe. Red and white striped warning posts indicate the limit of safe approach to a range area. Care must be taken when walking is permitted on the ranges – do not pick up any metal objects in, or even near, a firing range.

The Face of Exmoor

The Exmoor Coast

The interface between the sea and the land is one of Exmoor's most attractive features. For various reasons—geological, topographical, biological and historical—much of the coastline is undeveloped, and because of its National Park status, and through extensive National Trust ownership, is likely to remain so.

The geology of Exmoor is rarely assertive. On Dartmoor the hard underlying granite pokes through the surface in tors and outcrops. Exmoor is largely composed of softer sandstones and shales which are more easily eroded by weather, so that only where the sea is nibbling into the edge is one aware of much rock. This is particularly apparent at the Valley of Rocks, near Lynton, where in the geological past a valley has been captured by the sea. Perhaps only here is one brought face to face with the bones of the land. The height of the hills next to the coast, coupled with the relatively soft rock, has led to a hog's back type of cliff.

There is a lack of the kind of inlet which readily adapts to a harbour, and the hills behind were too steep for easy communications. In historic times, when Britain was at war with France and Spain the English Channel coast was strategically more important. Places like Dartmouth, Plymouth, Fowey and Falmouth not only had good natural harbours, but faced the 'right' way. Later, when it became fashionable to visit coastal watering places a level walking-out area, or promenade, became necessary, and Sidmouth, Exmouth, Teignmouth and Torquay developed on the south coast.

Some ship-borne trading was carried out between the small Exmoor ports of Combe Martin, Lynmouth, Porlock Weir and Minehead, mostly with ports across the Bristol Channel. Limestone and coal came in, and pit props, bark, umber and farm produce were exported. Small sailing craft even ran up on rough beaches like Heddon's Mouth, Woody Bay, Countisbury Cove and Glenthorne Beach to unload limestone and coal for the kilns which burnt the limestone to make quicklime, thus to lower the acidity of the Exmoor soil, but this trade ceased as commercially manufactured fertilizers became easier to obtain.

When the taste for romantic scenery developed in the last century discerning people began to visit the Exmoor coast, and Lynton and Lynmouth were the most popular destinations. At the same time the flourishing Bristol Channel paddle steamer business was partly compensating for the difficulties of road travel.

Nowhere else in England are there so many severe gradients on the roads. Lynmouth Hill is probably the worst, a 1:3 ascent with bends from a standing start. Countisbury Hill is longer, but straighter. Porlock has two winding roads heading west, and there is one from Porlock Weir. Where these are well-used routes escape roads are provided. Certainly one sees deep tyre marks in them sometimes, probably an indication of their usefulness. Cyclists are advised to dismount when descending the more precipitous slopes.

Countisbury Hill looking west towards Lynmouth.

Groyne at Porlock Bay, Exmoor.

Benign ownership has helped in the preservation of the coastline. The Acland family owned a vast chunk of north-west Somerset extending from the sea at Minehead Bluff to Exford Common. This is known as the Holnicote Estate and most of it was given to the National Trust in 1944 by Sir Richard Acland.

At Glenthorne, a considerable length of coast belonged to the Halliday family from the 1820s to the 1980s, but the house has now been sold. Much of the cliff land was bought by the National Trust who own long stretches all the way to the outskirts of Combe Martin.

The Exmoor coast is not a place for 'bucket and spade' holidays, but what it lacks in conventional seaside attractions it makes up for in wildlife, remoteness and wonderful unspoilt scenery.

THE EXMOOR WOODLANDS

When one has been visiting a place for years it is difficult to be objective about its character. You get involved in some aspect or other, and bias and preference begin to creep in. Certainly in any contest between Dartmoor and Exmoor, the former would win hands down on acreage of continuous open country, the number of prehistoric remains and visible rock! Exmoor, however, is not rivalled by its larger West Country neighbour in the size and quality of its woodlands—especially valley woodlands—and in having a glorious coastline.

Dartmoor's valley woodlands are mostly concentrated on the east and south-east side of the National Park, but don't make a great impact on the visitor compared with its other features. Only on the southern fringes of Exmoor between East Anstey Common and Blackmoor Gate is woodland in short supply, and this is well compensated by vast tracts in the north-east sector. Visitors going home from Exmoor remember the wooded combes above all else. There are 17,000 acres of woods in the Exmoor National Park; 10 per cent of the total land area.

Perhaps the most visited of valley woodland sites is Watersmeet, 1½ miles (2.4 km) upriver from Lynmouth. The area is typical of many others and is easily accessible. The valley sides were too steep for cultivation and settlement, so trees have probably always grown here. This is not to say that this is an ancient wildwood. Up to perhaps sixty or seventy years ago these slopes were managed by their owners. The best trees were used for building; the bark was sold for tanning; shorter poles were exported across the British Channel as pit props; and the smaller timber was used in the manufacture of charcoal or fencing or sold as firewood. The charcoal was made 'on site' and one can still come across charcoal burners' platforms, cut into the hillside wherever there have been woods for many years.

The trees are mostly oak, but ash, holly and beech are present too. The latter is unwelcome as a forest tree; nothing else will grow beneath a beech, so the species could in the course of time take over a woodland.

Because the trees grow on such steep rocky slopes the root system anchoring the trees is less efficient than if the trees were growing from good level ground. Every now and again the weather can flatten a swathe of trees, and such a storm hit Devon in December 1981. A blizzard struck the county and large compartments were uprooted in the Heddon Valley, at Woody Bay and near Watersmeet. The nature of the ground made extraction difficult, but the scars have mostly healed and replanting is beginning to show.

Commercial forestry is mostly in the eastern part of Exmoor, to the west and south of Dunster. Fortunately the plan to plant the Chains—the highest and most visible part of Exmoor's open country—with conifers in 1958 was defeated by public outcry. This proposal alerted opinion to what could happen, even in a National Park, and was the catalyst which led to the formation of the Exmoor Society in that year.

THE RED DEER

Anyone following the Exmoor walks described in this book is likely to come across Britain's largest animal, the red deer. During the fieldwork for this book I saw two groups of hinds, in

A microcosm of Exmoor woodland.

Horner Woods and near Withypool, but the walker is warned that quiet behaviour is necessary to get close. The animals are very shy and every sense is acute.

The visitor is also likely to come across one of the Exmoor hunts during the period mid-August to early November and from late November to the end of April. There is no mistaking the occasion. Beside any high level road a line of Land Rovers will have spawned binocular-hung, Barbour-coated country people who stand on the skyline intently looking in one direction. Join them, and you may see the hunt itself, some mounted pink-coated hunt officials, perhaps several hundred riding followers, and of course the hounds. Seeing the deer however, is a matter of luck.

So associated with Exmoor are the deer that the National Park's symbol is a stag's head with a full set of antlers. It is perhaps the stag's antlers even more than the animal's size which set the red deer apart from other deer species in Britain; there is a nobility about a good 'head'. But if the antlers are regal, as befits Britain's king of beasts, they are also transitory, growing from nothing in early spring when the old head is cast, to a full spread in August. Richard Jefferies, the nineteenth century naturalist, perceptively observed that the growth of a stag's antlers coincides with that of the bracken.

The antlers are not just a symbol of power. They are used by the animals to defend their appropriated groups of hinds at the time of the 'rut', the mating time between mid-October and mid-November. This is the time of great activity when the clash of horn against horn will sometimes alert the moorland walker to rival stags in combat, or the 'belling' or roaring, particularly at dusk or dawn, can frighten the unsuspecting visitor. That this primeval, threatening sound can be emitted by such a gentle-looking creature surprises everyone.

Hunting on Exmoor arouses strong emotions, and it seems you are either for it or against it. Supporters claim it is the best way to control the herds which could otherwise do unacceptable damage to crops. Opponents say that selective shooting would be less cruel.

Estimates of numbers are difficult to arrive at, but a figure of 700 or 800 may be near the mark. They tend to live their days in woodland, only coming out onto the moor or into the fields at dusk and dawn. Sometimes, while lying up in bracken during daylight hours, a toss of their antlers to deter the flies will give away their presence, and then the walker may have an opportunity to get close, provided he employs stealthy fieldcraft. If he does, he will be rewarded by one of England's most exciting natural spectacles.

Opposite: *Dartmoor—the largest open space in southern England.*

SELECTED WALKS IN THE NATIONAL PARKS OF DARTMOOR & EXMOOR

INTRODUCTION TO THE ROUTE DESCRIPTIONS

1. ACCESS (see page 170) — On all Dartmoor land registered as common there is now legal public access and on Exmoor *de facto* access on the open moorland exists. Routes make the most of this situation, and also follow public rights of way and permitted paths. Some cross areas where access agreements have been negotiated. Elsewhere, the routes have been walked for a long time without objection. Hence, it is not expected that any difficulties will be encountered. Local byelaws and regulations affecting the commons and access agreements areas must be respected and, in particular, 'short cuts' should not be taken that could cause annoyance to local people.

2. ASCENT — The amount of climbing involved in each route has been estimated from the Outdoor Leisure or Landranger Ordnance Survey maps and should be regarded as approximate only. In some route descriptions specific reference is made to the length and height of individual climbs.

3. CAR-PARKS — Most of the walks start from public car-parks. For other walks parking arrangements are suggested to prevent indiscriminate parking, which can be a great nuisance to local people.

Car break-ins can occur anywhere, even in a National Park. The police advise to take valuables with you or leave them at home; items of value are no longer safe hidden from view in the boot. When parking your vehicle, remember that it is illegal to drive more than 15 yards from the road onto the open moorland.

4. INTERESTING FEATURES ON THE ROUTE — The best position for seeing these is indicated both in the route descriptions and on the maps by *(1)*, *(2)*, etc.

5. LENGTH — These are strictly 'map miles' estimated from the Outdoor Leisure or Landranger maps; no attempt has been made to take into account any ascent or descent involved.

6. MAPS

The maps are drawn to a scale of 1:25 000 or 1:50 000 and all names are as given on the Outdoor Leisure or Landranger maps. Field boundaries in particular should be taken as a 'best description'. The maps have been drawn, in the main, so that the route goes from the bottom to the top of a page. The arrow on each map points to grid north. The scale of some small features has been slightly exaggerated for clarity. For easy cross-reference, the relevant Outdoor Leisure and Landranger sheets are indicated on each map.

7. ROUTE DESCRIPTION

The letters 'L' and 'R' stand for left and right respectively. Where these are used for changes of direction then they imply a turn of about 90° when facing in the direction of the walk. 'Half L' and 'half R' indicate a half-turn, i.e. approximately 45°, and 'back half L' or 'back half R' indicate three quarter-turns, i.e. about 135°. PFS stands for 'Public Footpath Sign', PBS for 'Public Bridleway Sign' and OS for 'Ordnance Survey'.

To avoid constant repetition, it should be assumed that all stiles and gates mentioned in the route description are to be crossed (unless there is a specific statement otherwise).

8. STANDARD OF THE ROUTES

The briefest examination of the route descriptions that follow will show that the routes described cover a wide range of both length and difficulty; some of the easy routes at least can be undertaken by a family party, with care, at most times of the year, while the hardest routes are only really suitable for experienced fellwalkers who are both fit and well-equipped. Any walker therefore who is contemplating following a route should make sure before starting that it is within their ability.

It is difficult in practice, however, to assess the difficulty of any route because it is dependent upon a number of factors and will in any case vary considerably from day to day, even during the day, with the weather. Any consideration of weather conditions must, of course, be left to the walker himself (but read the section on safety and weather first). Apart from that, it is probably best to attempt an overall assessment of difficulty based upon the length, amount of ascent and descent, problems of route-finding and finally, upon the roughness of the terrain. Dartmoor and Exmoor are not mountainous but they should never be under-estimated; the going underfoot can be very heavy. Each of the routes has been given a grading based upon a consideration of these factors. A general description of each grade follows:

Easy (1) Generally short walks (up to 6 miles, 9.7 km) over moderately easy ground with no problems of route-finding except in poor visibility. Progress is mostly over fairly gradual

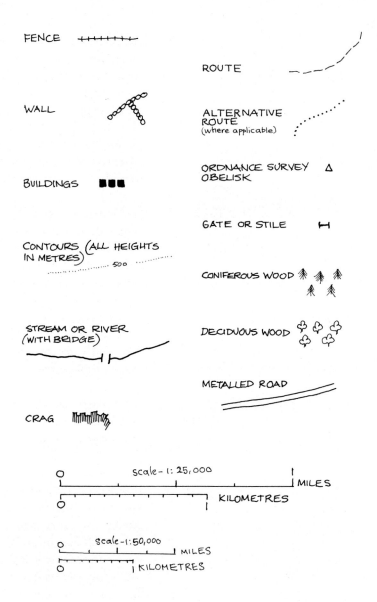

FIGURE 3 *Symbols used on detailed route maps.*

slopes with some short sections of more difficult ground. The paths may, however, sometimes run near steep slopes such as quarry edges; care should be taken here and amongst the moorland clitter.

Moderate (2) Rather longer walks (up to about 10 miles, 16 km) with some routes over paths but where most involve more difficult route-finding across moorland. Tor summits will be reached with climbing over steeper and rougher ground.

More strenuous (3) Longer walks (10–14 miles, 16–23 km on Dartmoor, and 14–23 miles, 22.5–37 km on Exmoor) with prolonged spells of climbing. Some rough ground calling for good route-finding ability, particularly in poor weather conditions.

Very strenuous (4) Only for the few if trying to complete in one day, and they involve long distances (over 15 miles on Dartmoor).

The walks are arranged in order of increasing difficulty in each Park, so that Routes 1 and 15 are the easiest and Routes 14 and 23 are the hardest. Finally, a summary of each walk is given at the head of each section, with information on the distance, amount of climbing and any special difficulties that will be met along the way. Several walks enter Ministry of Defence Firing Ranges on northern Dartmoor; firing times will need to be checked before embarking. (See section on the Ministry of Defence on Dartmoor.)

9. STARTING AND FINISHING POINTS

The majority of the routes are circular in order to avoid any problems with transport when the walk is completed. The location of each starting and finishing point is given by the number of the appropriate Landranger (1:50 000) map with a six-figure grid reference (see page 173); thus (55—854383) indicates a grid reference which can be found on Landranger sheet no. 55.

10. TIME FOR COMPLETION

The usual method of estimating the length of time needed for a walk is by Naismith's Rule: 'For ordinary walking allow one hour for every 3 miles (5 km) and add one hour for every 2000 feet (600 m) of ascent; for backpacking with a heavy load allow one hour for every 2½ miles (4 km) and one hour for every 1500 feet (450 m) of ascent.' However, for many this tends to be over-optimistic and it is better for each walker to form an assessment of his or her own performance over one or two walks. Naismith's Rule also makes no allowance for rest or food stops or for the influence of weather conditions.

1.1

BENCH TOR

STARTING AND FINISHING POINT
Venford Reservoir on the Holne to Hexworthy road. Car-park to the east of the dam (191/202-689709). 5 miles (8 km) west of Ashburton.
LENGTH
2¼ miles (4 km)
ASCENT
Mostly level walking

Bench Tor is a rugged climax to the River Dart's departure from the Dartmoor granite and from it are breath-taking views of the river some 500 feet (152 m) below. This easy walk follows the rock ridges of the tor, it penetrates the woods below and then follows a pipe-line track running above the Venford Brook back towards Venford Reservoir.

ROUTE DESCRIPTION (Map 1)

Follow a path uphill from the back of the car-park which offers good views over Venford Reservoir and Holne Moor. On reaching a banked-up leat (on R), which supplies water to the settlements at Stoke, continue straight on keeping the leat on the R. After a short distance go straight on along a wide path running beside the field boundaries on the R, and follow to the rock-crowned summit of Bench Tor *(1)*. In summer keep close to the wall on approaching the tor to avoid a large area of bracken on the L. Walk along the rock ridge to the northern pile—a distance of 500 yards (457 m).

From the tor go back half L and then R downslope to enter the wood below *(2)*. Continuing in the same direction go down amongst the trees to reach a waterworks pipe track. Turn L onto the track, edged by granite kerbs, and follow the Venford Brook (down on R) upstream to almost the perimeter fence of the treatment works. Here cut half L up the slope and, keeping the fence on the R, continue straight on to return to the road and car-park *(3)*.

A very pleasant round-reservoir walk, about 1 mile (1.6 km) in length, can be picked up by following the road over the dam (information board and toilets in the car-park at the far end on the R) and turn L through a gate in the perimeter fence; the walk allows a return to the starting point.

1 Bench Tor
Bench Tor is depicted as 'Benjay Tor' on the first edition OS one-inch map of 1809 and an old deed denotes a North and South Bench Tor. Looking down into the valley from the

28

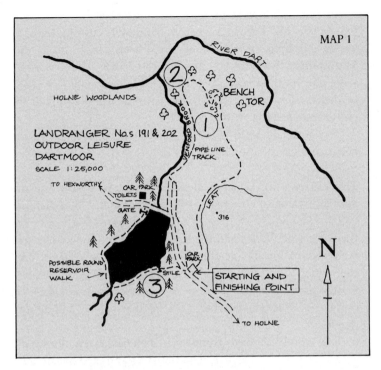

MAP 1

RIVER DART

HOLNE WOODLANDS

BENCH TOR

LANDRANGER No.s 191 & 202
OUTDOOR LEISURE
DARTMOOR
SCALE 1:25,000

VENFORD BROOK

PIPE LINE
TRACK

TO HEXWORTHY

CAR PARK
TOILETS

GATE

LEAT

·316

POSSIBLE ROUND
RESERVOIR
WALK

CAR
PARK

STILE

STARTING AND
FINISHING POINT

TO HOLNE

N

Bench Tor and the Double Dart Gorge.

A common moorland moss.

north pile, granite (L) gives way to metamorphic rock (R). Opposite is Mil Tor from where the old local custom, known as the 'Rolling of the Waggon Wheels' took place on Midsummer Day on and off until the 1950s. Here, wheels were sent on their way down to the river some 600 feet (183 m) below. Few ever reached the bottom, being stopped by clitter and trees in Miltor Wood.

The unusually loud noise of the river here is described as being the 'cry of the Dart'.

2 Holne Woodlands

The wooded slopes below Bench Tor are part of a Site of Special Scientific Interest, known as Holne Woodlands, which extends for 2557 acres (1035 ha) across both sides of the River Dart Valley and the River Webburn. The whole site is important for its ancient semi-natural oak woodland. On the higher valley slopes the trees become more stunted and scattered and the woodland gives way to open moorland—a mosaic of bracken, heather, bell heather, gorse and moor grasses.

The woodland bird population includes raven, buzzard, great spotted woodpecker, wood warbler and pied flycatcher. The woodland edges are frequented by redstart and, on the adjoining moorland, stonechat and whinchat breed. Far below, dipper and grey wagtail nest alongside the river. The river also provides suitable conditions for the spawning of salmon and trout.

The National Park Authority owns 175 acres (71 ha) of Holne Woods, on the south side of the valley running west from the tor. Up to about sixty-five years ago these woods were being commercially managed for charcoal, bark and firewood. That management having stopped, the woods today are predominantly of even-aged oak which are increasingly subject to die-back and windblow and, being unfenced against grazing livestock on the moor, regeneration is severely hindered. To ensure their survival as a major landscape and ecological feature, the National Park Authority is having to explore the most appropriate and acceptable methods of management.

3 Venford Reservoir

Venford Reservoir dam, built of Dartmoor granite from quarries nearby and at Merrivale, was completed in 1907. The reservoir was originally constructed to provide water for Paignton which was fast becoming a popular seaside resort. By 1925 this supply proved insufficient and further water had to be piped to the reservoir from the River Swincombe, a distance of 5 miles (8 km); the spillway where this water enters the reservoir can be seen close to the dam.

1.2

PEW TOR AND VIXEN TOR

STARTING AND FINISHING
POINT
Large car-park on the B3357 at the
top of Pork Hill on R 3 miles (5 km)
from Tavistock; 1½ miles (2.5 km)
west of Merrivale (191-531751).
LENGTH
3¼ miles (5 km)
ASCENT
Mostly level walking between
885–1040 ft (270–317 m) above sea
level.

This route offers wide unbroken views over much of south-west Dartmoor, Plymouth Sound and south east Cornwall and of the beautiful wood-and-torscape of the Walkham valley.

ROUTE DESCRIPTION (Map 2)

Head to the westernmost end of the car-park for the granite plinth which supports a brass-made depiction of the panorama ahead. This structure was erected by the Royal Town Planning Institute to commemorate the seventieth anniversary of the Institute and to contribute to the enjoyment of the countryside. Turn L from the car-park and continue straight on (due south) to pick up a well-defined track which is flanked on the R for a short distance by a series of large boulders. Continue straight over the leat and, where the track passes close to a field boundary wall on the R, bear L along a small path making for the leaning granite cross known as Windy Post, sometimes known as Beckamoor Cross. The faces of this chamfered cross look almost due north and south. Here several trans-Dartmoor packhorse tracks converge which linked the eastern border country towns of Chagford and Ashburton with Tavistock.

Cross over the Grimstone and Sortridge Leat next to where a branch leat leads off by the cross *(1)*. Continue straight on to Feather Tor which rises to 1028 feet (313 m) above sea level. The immense amount of clitter surrounding the tor indicates its primeval dimensions. Continue straight on to Pew Tor *(2)*, a prominent landmark from afar, crossing over the branch leat on the way and keeping this on the L thereafter.

After an exploration of the summit area go left downslope and follow a former cart track keeping a boundary wall on the R and Heckwood Tor above on the L. Pass Heckwood Quarry on the L, noticing a large, dressed granite block; this was shaped for the 1812 Plymouth Breakwater and was abandoned due to a flaw. Vixen Tor comes into view straight ahead.

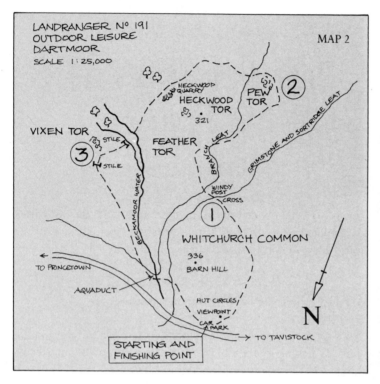

Cross over the Beckamoor Water at the ford and ascend the hill ahead for a stile leading into Vixen Tor Newtake. Go over the stile and go straight on up the hill keeping the rock pile immediately on the R *(3)*. The tor is on private land and permitted access to it has been granted provided that no fires are lit, no one camps here and dogs are not taken into the newtake. From the tor bear L, keeping your back to the Walkham Valley and leave the newtake by way of a stile provided by the National Park Authority in 1987. Continue straight on following Beckamoor Water upstream keeping the combe with its extensive evidence of tin streaming on the L. Go to the top of the gully whereupon a small aqueduct carries the Grimstone and Sortridge Leat over Beckamoor Water. Bear L and go over the lower, north slope of Barn Hill, cross over a leat diversion channel, keeping the main road on the R, and return to the car-park.

1 The Grimstone and Sortridge Leat

The Grimstone and Sortridge Leat was built some five centuries ago. Manor houses and farms are the main terminals and there are more delivery points on this leat than on any other on Dartmoor. The leat is taken from the River Walkham below Great Mis Tor and returns to the river 7 miles (11.3 km) further on. Running parallel with the leat,

Previous page: *Pew Tor from Feather Tor.*

Above: *The medieval Windy Post Cross, standing beside a 500-year-old leat.*

from its take-off point to the Windy Post, is a dry leat which is believed to have been cut in the 1870s to serve Tor Quarry. Local commoners objected to the scheme, which was subsequently aborted.

2 *Pew Tor*

Pew Tor stands some 1000 feet (305 m) above sea level. Here nature and man have created a wilderness of granite. On the summit pile are many shallow hollows known as rock basins. There were those, particularly during the first half of the last century, who believed that such phenomena were Druidical Seats of Judgement. Rock basins are, in fact, a natural formation produced by the combined effects of frost, wind and water.

3 *Vixen Tor*

Vixen Tor is a spectacular rock pile of ramparts and bastions overlooking the River Walkham valley. It is the highest tor on Dartmoor from the ground to its top—93 feet (29.3 m) on its south face. Writers in the last century noted that, from the north, this granite outcrop 'resembles the Egyptian Sphynx in a mutilated state'; today, and somewhat more prosaically, moormen see the anthropomorphic northern face as 'an old man who has turned his back on his wife'.

1.3

MERRIVALE—KING'S TOR—SWELL TOR AND FOGGIN TOR

STARTING AND FINISHING
POINT
Car-park in a roadside quarry on L
side of B3357, as approach
Merrivale Bridge from Princetown
(191-553750); 3 miles (5 km) west
of Two Bridges, 4½ miles (7.2 km)
east of Tavistock.
LENGTH
4 miles (6.5 km)
ASCENT
Mostly level walking between
1050–1312 ft (320–400 m) above
sea level.

This walk allows an exploration of the prehistoric stone rows, stone circle, cairns and standing stone on Long Ash Hill, which together represent one of the finest groups of ancient monuments on Dartmoor. The walk follows for much of its length the now-closed Yelverton to Princetown Railway which was built in 1881 along the trackbed of an earlier line—a horse-truck tramway (the Plymouth and Dartmoor Railway) used for transporting granite from the quarries.

ROUTE DESCRIPTION (Map 3)

From the east end of the car-park, walking with your back to Merrivale Quarry, head off over the moor, half R, in the direction of North Hessary Tor mast. After some 250 yards (229 m) head half R again over the crest of Long Ash Hill. A prehistoric sanctuary (1) comprising kistvaens, a stone circle, a menhir, cairns and three stone rows—two double and one single—comes into view.

Keeping to the L of the rows cross over a leat via a small granite slab to prevent bank erosion. Follow the southern double stone row down, almost due west, to its far end—a distance of some 280 yards (256 m). From here go half L passing a cairn circle, and go to the stone circle and the fine menhir.

From the menhir bear L keeping the boundary wall to the R. Follow a path keeping above (L) of the bluff for a short distance and then cut down R to follow a path through the tinners' spoil heaps keeping the stream on the R; the going can be boggy here. Cross the stream (the Pila Brook) by the ford and follow the boundary wall on the R up the slope. Where the wall bends markedly to the R continue straight on up the hill to pick up the track bed of the former Yelverton and Princetown Railway,

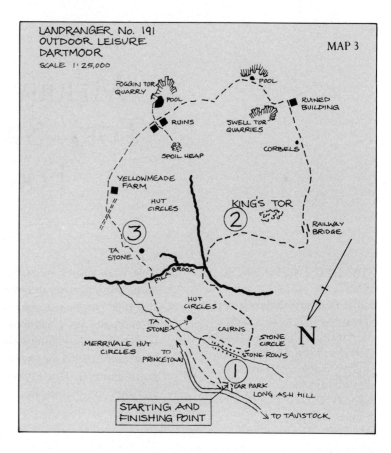

LANDRANGER No. 191
OUTDOOR LEISURE
DARTMOOR
SCALE 1:25,000

MAP 3

FOGGIN TOR QUARRY
POOL
POOL
RUINED BUILDING
RUINS
SWELL TOR QUARRIES
CORBELS
SPOIL HEAP
YELLOWMEADE FARM
HUT CIRCLES
KING'S TOR
RAILWAY BRIDGE
③
TA STONE
PILA BROOK
②
N
HUT CIRCLES
TA STONE
CAIRNS
STONE CIRCLE
MERRIVALE HUT CIRCLES
TO PRINCETOWN
STONE ROWS
①
CAR PARK
LONG ASH HILL
TO TAVISTOCK

STARTING AND FINISHING POINT

which was built for most of its length on an earlier line, the Plymouth and Dartmoor Railway (P & DR) *(2)*.

The track forks as it swings L round King's Tor; here take the R fork along the P & DR for extensive views over the Walkham valley. Follow the track round to the L and, on approaching a fine granite railway bridge, cross over the Yelverton and Princetown Railway track and turn R for Swell Tor Sidings. Continue straight on along this track bed to Swelltor Quarries passing abandoned granite corbels on the L. On this track are many sleepers, some with their retaining bolts—watch where you put your feet. On reaching a ruined building (R), opposite the mouth of the quarry, turn L uphill keeping the quarry entrance down on the L. Keep over to the R to avoid encountering the quarry edge. On reaching the first level half way up the hill bear R passing the spoil heaps radiating out from the side of the tor. Continue along the track here bending round to the L, passing two smaller quarries (one water-filled) and their accompanying spoil heaps on the R. If the weather should become misty, to avoid climbing above Swelltor Quarries continue straight on along the track from the ruined building and contour L round the hillside.

Left: *Abandoned granite corbels near Swell Tor sidings.*

Following page: *Foggintor Quarries. Several considerable ruins still survive.*

Go along the track in the direction of Foggintor Quarries; granite sleepers with bolts can be seen along this stretch. Where the track and a path intersect, turn R and follow the path towards the quarries. On reaching the Yelverton and Princetown Railway track in a shallow cutting, cut straight across and continue on the path. At the next track bear L and go to the ruined buildings. At the largest ruin on the L, with its massive granite blockwork, bear L passing between the two walls of the building and follow the spoil heap to its far end, being wary of ironwork jutting slightly out of the ground at regular intervals. The views west and north include King's Tor, Cox Tor, Long Ash Hill, Staple Tors, Roos Tor and Great Mis Tor. Below lies Yellowmeade Farm. Retrace your steps to the track and cut straight over following the path leading into the quarry, the sheer sides of which reflect in a small lake. The quarry can be explored by following the path round to the L. Here is the stillness of abandonment; echoes of blasting, chiselling, hauling and the voices of quarrymen have given way once more to raven croak and buzzard mew.

Retrace your steps and go R along the track and pass Yellowmeade Farm (on L). On reaching the final stone-walled enclosure on the L continue straight on for about 20 yards (18 m) beyond the junction with the farm track and bear L. Pass an oval-shaped prehistoric enclosure and go straight on downslope to a standing stone which marks a medieval route across Dartmoor *(3)*. Go half R and continue on in the direction of Four Winds—an isolated clump of beech trees which used to be the site of a school serving quarry workers' children. Cross over the tinning gullies and then a small stream—it may be necessary to walk upstream to cross over safely. Continue on

over the hill, in the direction of Great Staple Tor, keeping Four Winds on the R. Cross over the leat where appropriate and keeping this well on the L continue in the same direction until approaching the stone rows once more. From here bear half R in the direction of Merrivale Quarry. With a Tavistock to Ashburton marker stone immediately on the L, in line with King's Tor, go half R passing some large prehistoric hut circles and inside one of the low-walled prehistoric enclosures is a granite apple crusher abandoned by the hand that made it, possibly because of an unacceptable flaw. Continue straight on in the direction of Merrivale Quarry to return to the car-park.

1 *Long Ash Hill Prehistoric Monuments*
The prehistoric monuments on the level plain of Long Ash Hill, near Merrivale may be a prehistoric sanctuary used for burials and ceremonies by several generations. Two double stone rows set 30 yards (27.4 m) apart run parallel to each other in an almost east–west orientation. These rows thus form a prehistoric 'avenue'—a unique feature on Dartmoor.

2 *The Plymouth and Dartmoor Railway*
The Plymouth and Dartmoor Railway (P & DR) was the brainchild of Sir Thomas Tyrwhitt. He was private secretary to George, Prince Regent, and was granted lands on Dartmoor in the Princetown area by the Prince in 1785. His ambition was to transform the high plateaux of Dartmoor, which in his eyes appeared as useless waste, into a vast prairie growing cereals and grass. He founded the community of Prince's Town (now Princetown) at a height of about 1345 feet (410 m) above sea level, and in 1819 he submitted a tramroad plan to Plymouth Chamber of Commerce and royal assent for this horse-driven railroad was given in 1821. This was to be Devon's first iron railroad and was opened on 26 September 1823.

3 *A medieval road*
A medieval trans-moorland packhorse track from Tavistock to Ashburton remained in use down the centuries until it was superseded by the turnpike road of 1792. Inscribed guide-posts—so-called 'T and A Stones'—were erected along the route, the initials 'T' and 'A' facing the appropriate town. By an Act of Parliament dated 1696 justices could enforce the erection of guide stones on roads; the 'T' and 'A' stones were sponsored in 1699 by Plymouth Corporation, which paid £2 for them to be put up, to help those travelling over Dartmoor find their way towards the city. These stones may have replaced an earlier series.

Shipley Bridge—Avon Dam—Eastern White Barrow—Black Tor

STARTING AND FINISHING POINT
Shipley Bridge (202-681629). Large car-park; information board and toilets. 2½ miles (4 km) north north west of South Brent. Narrow lane approach, proceed with caution.

LENGTH
4½ miles (7 km)

ASCENT
One steep climb: 1 mile (1.5 km), ascent 505 ft (154 m) from the Avon Dam to Eastern White Barrow.

This walk, of moderate length, collides with the twentieth century on its approach to the Avon Dam and meets with more subtle exploitation of the moorland in the form of a prehistoric farmstead and village. For the second half of its length this is a high moorland walk and it should not be attempted in bad weather.

Route Description (Map 4)

From the car-park pass the toilet block (on L) and continue straight on along the Water Authority access road (vehicular access to authorized vehicles only) northwards following the River Avon (on R) upstream. Within a short distance, just before a side road leads off and back to the L to the Avon Filtration Works is an inscribed granite block—the Hunters' Stone *(1)* on L. Continue upstream along the road passing the grounds and foundations of Brent Moor House (L) *(2)*. From here the road emerges out into open country flanked by Black Tor on the L and Dockwell Ridge on the R. Cross over the road bridge to continue on up the valley with the river now on the L. On the approach to Woolholes the valley bottom becomes flatter and broader. The river soon becomes confined again in Long-a-Traw where legend has it that a certain John Dill, a small-time smuggler, jumped the river here on horseback, while being pursued by the farmer from whom he had taken the horse.

Avon Dam now lies ahead *(3)*. The road here bears L crossing back over the river; follow the road to its end at the dam. Continue half L up the steep slope to the western end of the dam and, from here, go L heading straight on up the slope over open moorland keeping the reservoir down on the R. Soon, the

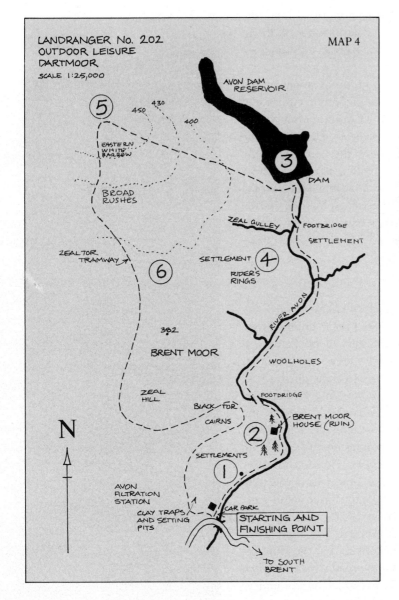

Map caption in image:
LANDRANGER No. 202
OUTDOOR LEISURE
DARTMOOR
SCALE 1:25,000

MAP 4

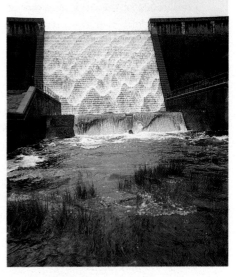

Above: *The Avon Dam.*

Following page: *A china clay settling pit above Shipley Bridge.*

huge—almost submarine-like—shape of Eastern White Barrow comes into view, but also notice beyond Zeal Gulley the prehistoric settlement of Rider's Rings *(4)*. Continue straight on for the prehistoric burial mound *(5)*.

From this summit go half L down the hill over Broad Rushes, keeping the headwater of the Bala Brook on the R. Head for a marked track running down the hillside. Turn L onto the track which is the trackbed of the nineteenth-century Zeal Tor Tramway in which peat was brought down from the moor to Shipley Bridge in horse-drawn trucks, and, which was later in the same century used to facilitate china clay extraction at Petre's Pit at the head of the Bala Brook *(6)*. Continue on down the track until Black Tor is immediately on the L and the confluence of the Middle Brook and the Bala Brook is on the R. Go L straight over the plain to Black Tor passing a mound—a ruined cairn—en route.

Go back half R from the tor passing a group of stones on the L which comprise a prehistoric settlement of hut circles and pound set within its own field system. Continue straight on until the Water Works filtration plant is visible. Descend to the Water Works road, cross over, and follow the path beside the wall (R) and then go L to explore the rectangular and circular pits which once served a clayworks here. Continue on down the slope to the road and car-park keeping a ruined building on the L. On either side of the road are further remains of the former clayworks which adopted the site of an abandoned peat-distilling works.

1 *The Hunters' Stone*

Mohun Harris who resided at Brent Moor House towards the end of the nineteenth century instigated the Hunters' Stone in memory of past huntsmen and Masters of Foxhounds of the Dartmoor Hunt. The Shipley Bridge area was one of the many Meets of the Hunt. The first inscriptions on the rock were the work of Billy Knott, a sculptor and fiddler, and include the names of 'Paul Treby', 'Trelawney', 'Bulteel' and 'Carew', together with Mohun Harris's initials. Paul Treby was never a Master of the Hunt but ran his own hounds from near Plympton in the eighteenth century. He did, however, give his hounds to Mr John Bulteel of Flete whose son John Crocker Bulteel acquired them in 1801; the latter became the first Master of the Dartmoor Hunt in 1827.

The Dartmoor National Park Committee was approached by a sub-committee of the Hunt in 1954 so that the Hunters' Stone could be re-sited further from the road which was then servicing the construction of the Avon Dam. The Committee allocated £25 for the job to be carried out.

2 *Brent Moor House*

The ruins of Brent Moor House are all that remain of the Meynell family residence built in the nineteenth century. The Meynells' estate of 3000 acres (1214 ha) stretched far over the southern moors. Attempts were made to enclose some of the moor but local commoners objected.

Mohun Harris subsequently used the building as a hunting-lodge and it was during this time that the rhododendrons which now adorn the valley here were planted. At the turn of the century the house was leased to Rear Admiral John Tuke who was at that time Captain of the Dockyard at Devonport,

Plymouth. Before the Second World War it became a Youth Hostel but apparently was not successful as such—such a place today, no doubt, would be. From late 1954 until 1957 it was used as a dormitory for the Water Board workers engaged in the construction of the Avon Dam. It then lay empty for ten years and was vandalized and, in 1968, the Royal Marines blew up what was left.

3 *The Avon Dam Reservoir*

The Avon Dam Reservoir was first mooted in 1948 and a public enquiry was held in 1949; the National Park was not to be designated until two years later. The dam took three years to construct and was completed in 1957 for the then South Devon Water Board.

4 *Rider's Rings*

Rider's Rings is a prehistoric 'village' enclosure. It lies at a height of about 1200 feet (366 m) above sea level and consists of two parts which together comprise about 6 acres (2.4 ha). It is one of the largest known on the moor and contains about thirty-six hut circles (prehistoric round houses) some of which are attached to the inside of the enclosure wall. Here, too, are numerous sub-rectangular 'yards' or stock pens. The two parts of this enclosure suggest an expanding community.

5 *Eastern White Barrow*

Eastern White Barrow was recorded at the perambulation of the Forest of Dartmoor in 1240 as *Ester Whyteburghe*. This immense prehistoric stone cairn marks a burial dating to about 2000 BC and is about 250 feet (76 m) long and some 36 feet (11 m) high. The 'tower' on the top of the cairn was probably a later addition.

6 *Zeal Tor Tramway*

Commercial exploitation of peat from Dartmoor began towards the end of the eighteenth century, the product being brought off the moors by packhorse trains. On 11 June 1846 the Duchy of Cornwall (the landowner) granted a licence to L. H. Davy and William Wilkins of Totnes for 'cutting manufacturing and vending peat and peat charcoal.' The licence also allowed the building of a tramway (the Zeal Tor Tramway) for delivering the peat to the treatment works at Shipley Bridge from the ties at Redlake. The venture sadly proved unsuccessful and the factory was closed by 1850.

The tramway returned to partial use in 1872 when the Brent Moor Clay Company purchased all stock and equipment and converted the redundant naphtha works into clay-dries. The tramway was used to carry materials and moorland clay pit workers to and from Shipley Bridge.

LUSTLEIGH CLEAVE

STARTING AND FINISHING
POINT
Trendlebere Down, 2 miles (3.2 km)
north north west of Bovey Tracey on
the Manaton road (191-784793).
From Bovey Tracey continue on the
road passing the main entrance to
Yarner Wood National Nature
Reserve (L) and after going over the
cattle grid follow the road round to L
and park immediately on R on a small
parking area on the edge of the
common.
LENGTH
7 miles (11 km)
ASCENT
Three short climbs all about ⅓ mile
(0.5 km) in length:
ascent 312 ft (95 m) to lower slopes
of Sharpitor;
197 ft (60 m) to Hunter's Tor;
180 ft (55 m) on return to car-park
on Trendlebere Down.

This walk follows public rights of way for its entire length, all being well waymarked. These paths offer beautiful riverside walking including a short detour to Horsham Steps where the river strews its way under and round moss-covered boulders. It follows the side of the Cleave, graced by birch trees, and up along its boldest ridge from which there are spectacular views. Woodland and scrub constitute a great fire risk in the Cleave; guard against all risk of fire.

ROUTE DESCRIPTION (Map 5)

From the car-park walk down the track running alongside the woodland boundary on the R. This is tarmaced in places and is the 'Old Manaton Road', now unsuitable for vehicular use. Where the track levels out we pass part of the Bovey Valley Woodlands National Nature Reserve (R) *(1)*. Continue along the track amongst the oak, holly, hazel, and birch. Ignore a path on the R and go straight on until reaching the Becka Brook. Here, cross over the footbridge (PFS) on R. Turn R and follow path which soon heads L as it contours round the wooded Houndtor Ridge.

We now enter the Bovey Valley. Continue on upstream, keeping the river on the R, for about 1 mile (1.6 km). At the footbridge (R)—comprising two trunks placed end-to-end and with handrail—cross over the river. Follow the bridlepath straight on up the side of the Cleave (PBS 'Lustleigh'). On reaching a path junction, ignore turning on the R, and continue straight on up slope (PBS 'Lustleigh via Hammerslake'). A short steep climb leads to another path junction. Here turn L (PBS 'Foxworthy Bridge') and follow the path down the side of the Cleave keeping Sharpitor Rocks on the R.

On approaching the valley bottom a footpath leads to the L (PFS 'Horsham for Manaton and Water'). A small detour here of 200 yards (183 m) is worth taking to Horsham Steps *(2)*. Retrace steps to continue along the public bridlepath to Foxworthy, passing Foxworthy Mill (L). At Foxworthy Bridge

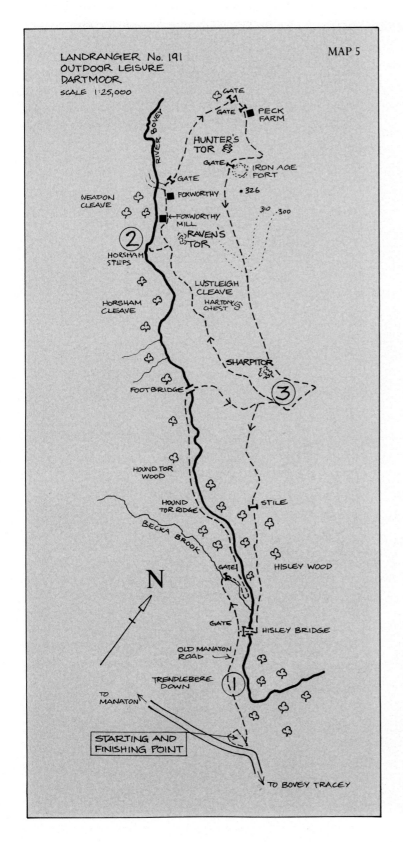

LANDRANGER No. 191
OUTDOOR LEISURE
DARTMOOR
SCALE 1:25,000

MAP 5

GATE
GATE
PECK FARM
HUNTER'S TOR
GATE
IRON AGE FORT
RIVER BOVEY
GATE
NEADON CLEAVE
FOXWORTHY
•326
FOXWORTHY MILL
310 •300
RAVEN'S TOR
②
HORSHAM STEPS
LUSTLEIGH CLEAVE
HARTON CHEST
HORSHAM CLEAVE
SHARPITOR
③
FOOTBRIDGE
HOUND TOR WOOD
N
HOUND TOR RIDGE
STILE
BECKA BROOK
HISLEY WOOD
GATE
GATE
HISLEY BRIDGE
OLD MANATON ROAD
TRENDLEBERE DOWN
①
TO MANATON
STARTING AND FINISHING POINT
TO BOVEY TRACEY

Opposite: The River Bovey in Lustleigh Cleave.

bear R following the track (PBS) 'Peck Farm and Road Nr Barnecourt') which swings L in front of dwellings at Foxworthy. Go through a gate and continue on the track until it ends on a farm drive. Go through the gate, turn R and follow the drive up to Peck Farm. Keeping the farmhouse on the L go through a gate (PBS) and walk up the L side of the field. Go L at the top and follow the path which swings half back R to Hunters' Tor.

Go through the gate on reaching Hunter's Tor noticing the subtle low ramparts of the Iron Age fort here on the L. Continue straight on along the ridge, passing the outcrops of Harton Chest (down on R), to Sharpitor *(3)*. Here, keep on the path running alongside the wall (L) and follow down through the wood keeping the tor on the R. Ignore a small path leading to a stile on the L, and near the bottom of the hill, by a gate, go R (PBS 'Clam Bridge/Horsham Steps/Heaven's Gate/Lustleigh and Hisley Bridge'). With Sharpitor Rocks again in view on the R keep to the lower L path and follow down to the next path junction (which we encountered earlier). Continue straight on down the hill (PBS 'Manaton via Water') to the next path junction. Here go L (PBS 'Lustleigh via Pethybridge') and continue straight on. Where the path forks take the R fork for Hisley Bridge. After a short distance go over the stile into the wood and continue on down to the river. At the river turn R and go over the arched packhorse bridge (PBS). Go through the gate and turn L (waymarked 'Nr Holne Brake'). Continue on up the 'Old Manaton Road' to return to the car parking area.

1 Bovey Valley
The Bovey Valley Site of Special Scientific Interest includes most of the Bovey Valley National Nature Reserve and extends for some 646 acres (265 ha). The Site comprises a large area of semi-natural broadleaved woodland, the whole of Lustleigh Cleave and extends up the Becka Brook valley beyond Becka Falls. The River Bovey flows over Dartmoor granite at the north end of the Cleave and on to more easily eroded slates and shales; the junction is marked by rapids.

2 Horsham Steps
Horsham Steps is a curious river crossing-place formed by a number of moss-strewn granite boulders, so close together that the river finds a way underneath them unless in flood.

3 The Nut Crackers stone
On the Ordnance Survey Map Sharpitor has a reference to the Nut Crackers logan stone. This huge rocking stone spectacularly overhung the Cleave until, in 1951, it was pushed off down into the valley below by vandals. In an attempt to heave it back, it fell further and broke into pieces.

Opposite: *The view north from Hunter's Tor.*

2.6

THE TEIGN VALLEY—STEPS BRIDGE TO CHAGFORD

STARTING POINT
Steps Bridge (191-803883), on B3212
4½ miles (7 km) north east of
Moretonhampstead and 7 miles (11
km) south west of Exeter. Car-park
and toilets here and a National Park
Information Centre (minimum
operating period—Easter–end of
October).
FINISHING POINT
The town centre, Chagford.
LENGTH
8½ miles (13.5 km)
ASCENT
One climb: ½ mile (0.8 km), ascent
413 ft (126 m) to near the hunting
gate, by Drewston Common, above
Fingle Bridge.

This off-the-moorland walk follows the River Teign upstream from Steps Bridge, on the north east boundary of the National Park, to the ancient market and stannary town of Chagford. It is possible to utilize an infrequent local bus service from Chagford to Exeter for a return to Steps Bridge, or use this service to start your journey from Exeter.

ROUTE DESCRIPTION (Maps 6—8)

From the car-park turn L onto B3212 and, taking care of traffic, cross Dunsford Bridge which spans the River Teign (1). Just beyond the bridge turn L through a gate to enter Meadhaydown Wood (2). Follow the path to the L (PBS 'County Road Nr Clifford Bridge'). Pass the weir and leat take-off point on the L. Within a short distance a Devon Trust for Nature Conservation information board, beautifully illustrated, will be encountered and this depicts the great variety of wildlife that can be found in the reserve which extends along the valley for 2 miles (3.2 km). Fork R along the public right-of-way (PBS) if the riverside path is temporarily closed to allow the restoration of eroded areas, otherwise fork L along the Daffodil Walk which follows the edge of the river. Further signs may ask you to follow the public path which runs parallel to this Walk.

At the far end of Dunsford Wood the path emerges from the trees onto a large level open area. The popularity of the area for walking and riding has necessitated a temporary diversion of the bridlepath (summer 1987) to enable the National Trust to carry out re-seeding. Continue on in the same direction, running parallel with the bridlepath, until reaching the far end of the nature reserve. Here, follow the path which swings half R through a group of trees. Cross over a wooden footbridge and

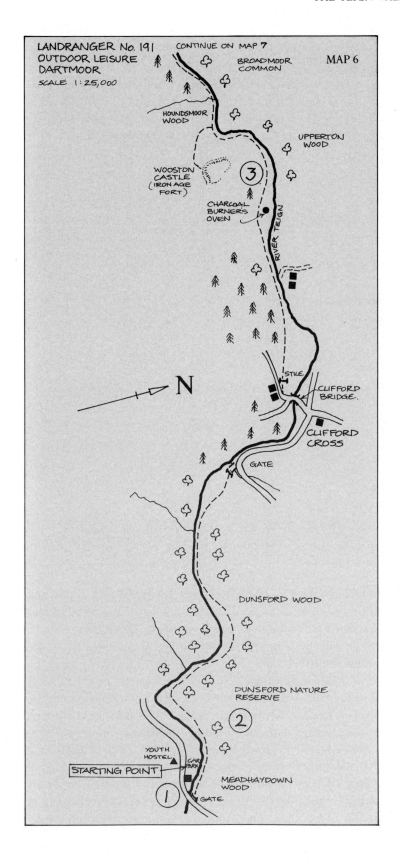

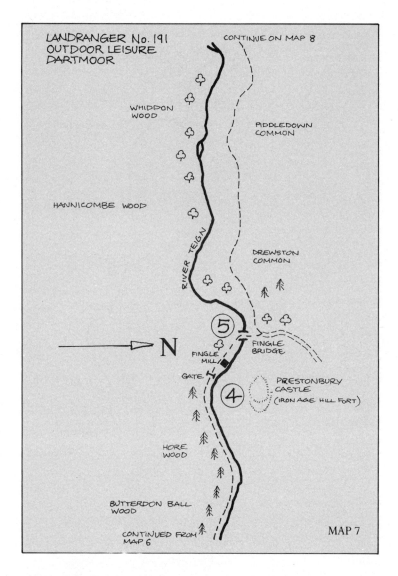

go through the gate which leads onto Boyland Road. Turn L and follow the lane to Clifford Bridge, bearing L at Clifford Cross (waymarked 'To path to Fingle Bridge'). Cross over Clifford Bridge and, ignoring the turning on the L, continue on up the hill for about 100 yards (91 m). Cross over the stile by a gate on the R (PFS 'Fingle Bridge'). A Fountain Forestry notice reminds us of the risk of fire in these woods. The route now follows the River Teign (on R) to Fingle Bridge. The path runs through working forests and can be muddy in places.

By Seaman's Borough look out for the rusty remains of a charcoal burner's oven on the R *(3)*. Continuing on for a further ⅓ mile (0.5 km) a National Park Authority information board on the L marks the point where a steep permitted path leads up to the out-of-view prehistoric hill fort of Wooston Castle.

River Teign Gorge bedrock—not granite, but Carboniferous sedimentary rocks.

Continue along the valley bottom here (unless feeling very energetic) and pass a craggy spur projecting from Broadmoor Common on the R.

After a further ¾ mile (1.2 km) the spur on which another fort is sited—Prestonbury Castle—comes dramatically into view (R) *(4)*. Go through the gate just beyond this spur and take the R fork for about 75 yards (69 m). Here are the substantial remains of Fingle Mill. The riverside meadow on the southern side of Fingle Bridge is the subject of an Access Agreement between the National Park Authority and the owners, under the terms of which the public has free access onto what would otherwise be private land. Continue straight on, keeping the car parking area on the L. Turn R to cross Fingle Bridge itself *(5)*.

From this famous Dartmoor beauty spot take the road for

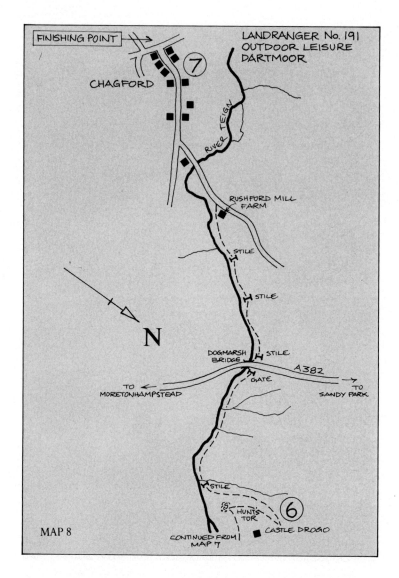

FINISHING POINT

LANDRANGER No. 191
OUTDOOR LEISURE
DARTMOOR

CHAGFORD ⑦

RIVER TEIGN

RUSHFORD MILL
FARM

STILE

STILE

N

DOGMARSH
BRIDGE

STILE

A382

GATE

TO ←
MORETONHAMPSTEAD

TO →
SANDY PARK

STILE

HUNTS
TOR

⑥

CASTLE DROGO

MAP 8

CONTINUED FROM
MAP 7

about 200 yards (183 km) and turn L onto the Hunter's Path. (PBS to Hunter's Path Nr Drogo Castle and Drewsteignton); do not take the Fisherman's Path along the river. After a steep climb the effort is soon rewarded with extensive views over the Teign Gorge; Hore Wood and Charles Wood clearly show the effects of coniferization in a broad-leaved landscape setting. At the next path junction bear L (PBS 'Hunter's Path Rd nr Drogo Castle and to the Fisherman's Path'). At the Hunting Gate continue straight on. Ahead, on the opposite side of the valley, well above the present-day treeline, is the Iron Age hill fort of Cranbrook Castle.

At the next path junction continue straight on for Sharp Tor; do not bear R for Drewsteignton. From this rugged tor, which rises almost from the valley bottom itself, are extensive views of

Near Fingle Mill weir.

the gorge and to Chagford and North Dartmoor beyond. It is possible to leave the path to the R, soon after the tor, for Castle Drogo *(6)*. Continue straight on (PBS 'Hunter's Path') to Hunt's Tor (erroneously named Hunter's Tor on OS maps). On the approach to Hunt's Tor we cross the boundary between the granite of high Dartmoor (to the west) and the sedimentary rocks of the Carboniferous Culm Measures (to the east).

From Hunt's Tor at the extreme western edge of the gorge follow a path down to the R keeping Castle Drogo above on the R. At the next path junction bear L along a track (PFS) passing the thatched dwellings at Combe. At the river bear R keeping the river on the L (PFS). However, a slight detour to the L along the Fisherman's Path, will take you to an iron bridge spanning the river and to a massive weir; otherwise bear R, go over a wooden footbridge, through a gate and continue along the riverside path through the meadows to Dogmarsh Bridge. The view back to the gorge and castle should not be missed.

On reaching the Moretonhampstead to Whiddon Down road go through the gate; we now leave the National Trust's Castle Drogo Estate. Cross straight over and follow path (PFS 'Chagford via Rushford Mill') running close to the river. On approaching Rushford Mill (a farm) Chagford comes into view flanked by the bracken slopes of Meldon Hill. A notice at the farm reminds us that this is a 'working farmyard—please pass straight through to the lane'. At the lane turn L and follow to Chagford passing the swimming pool and crossing over Rushford Bridge. At the top of the hill at a T junction go R for Chagford town centre (7).

1 *Dunsford Bridge*

Steps (Dunsford) Bridge dates from 1810. It replaced a bridge which was built in 1700 after two people were swept to their deaths from the original stepping-stones. These stones now form a weir upstream of the bridge. The weir was constructed to divert water to a leat which supplied a flour mill later to become an edge-tool factory. This factory, after one hundred years, is still in operation specializing in the manufacture of cutting hooks. Work began in 1987 to restore the leat.

2 *Dunsford Nature Reserve*

Dunsford Nature Reserve has been managed since 1965 by the Devon Trust for Nature Conservation. The 140 acre (56 ha) reserve includes Meadhaydown Woods which are owned by the National Trust. These woods, together with St Thomas Cleave and Bridford Wood (both also owned by the National Trust) form the Teign Valley Woods Site of Special Scientific Interest. The area is a fine example of upland oak and hazel woodland lying on the eastern fringes of Dartmoor. Dogs must be kept on a lead while walking through the reserves.

3 *Teign Valley Woods*

The earliest available maps showing some of the Teign Valley Woods were produced in 1790 when the land was part of the Earl of Devon's estate. It seems that the total woodland area was less extensive than today—the area around Wooston Castle was open common and much of the area south of Clifford Bridge was farmland. The 1840 Parish Tithe Map shows a similar situation.

4 *Prestonbury Castle*

Prestonbury Castle is a late prehistoric (Iron-Age) defensive

Opposite: Overlooking Fingle Bridge from Drewston Common.

site and occupies a dramatic position overlooking the gorge of the River Teign. It lies just over ½ mile (0.6 km) as the crow flies from Cranbrook Castle and 1 mile (1.6 km) from Wooston Castle, both on the south side of the valley. Together they represent a formidable group of defended sites on north-eastern Dartmoor. These and other small hill forts on the fringes of Dartmoor suggest a continued use of the uplands for settlement and grazing in the later first millenium.

5 *Fingle Bridge*

For over one hundred years tourists and local people have come to the famous Dartmoor beauty spot of Fingle Bridge. Local carriage owners brought parties from Chagford and from further away places such as Newton Abbot, Okehampton, Exeter and Crediton. The arrival of the railway to Moretonhampstead in 1866 (closed in 1959) brought more admiring visitors. The car has kept up the momentum.

6 *Castle Drogo*

Castle Drogo was the last 'castle' to be built in England. It was built between 1910 and 1930 for a Mr Drewe who had made his fortune in the grocery business. He chose this site partly because of its commanding position above the Teign Valley and because of the name of the nearby village Drewsteignton—the name implying a historical connection with his own family. Sir Edwin Lutyens was the architect. The Drewe family donated the castle and the 611-acre (247 ha) estate to the National Trust in 1974. The castle, garden and immediate area are open to the public from 1 April to 31 October every day from 11 am to 6 pm.

7 *Chagford*

For 200 years before AD 1300 Chagford slowly developed as a small marketing centre for nearby hill farmers. In 1185 a reference to Chagford tinners illegally smelting tin shows that tin working was taking place in the area. In 1305 Chagford was listed in a Tinners' Charter as one of several coinage towns for the tinners of Devon. Chagford thus became a Stannary Town where tin from north-east Dartmoor was weighed, tested for quality, stamped and then had duty paid on it. Disputes were resolved in its Stannary Court. With the decline of this industry, the eighteenth century saw farming dominating the scene and a local woollen industry reached its peak in the mid-nineteenth century. During Victorian times Chagford's tourist trade, still important today, began to develop. James Perrott, from about 1854 to his death in 1895, became a famous Dartmoor guide helping visitors to enjoy the surrounding countryside. His four sons carried on the guiding tradition throughout the Edwardian period.

HAY TOR AND HOUND TOR

STARTING AND FINISHING
POINT
Small car-park on east side of Saddle
Tor, off the main Bovey Tracey to
Widecombe-in-the-Moor road (191-
754764). 4 miles (6.4 km) west of
Bovey Tracey, 2.5 miles (4 km) east of
Widecombe-in-the-Moor.
LENGTH
6¼ miles (10 km)
ASCENT
Two climbs: about 250 yards
(229 m), ascent 188 ft (57 m)
to the summit of Hay Tor;
⅓ mile (0.5 km), ascent 197 ft (60 m)
from Becka Brook on approach to
Houndtor deserted settlement site.

The tors on the most eastern moorland block of the National Park dramatically reveal Dartmoor's granite face. The familiar outlines of Haytor Rocks, Saddle Tor and the nearby Rippon Tor can be seen on the skyline from many parts of south and east Devon. Hay Tor attracts many thousands of visitors each year and it and the surrounding Down (1089 acres, 441 ha) have, since 1975, been owned by the National Park Authority.

The Tor and the nearby Low Man offer the best climbing routes on Dartmoor.

ROUTE DESCRIPTION (Map 9)

Facing Hay Tor, go uphill half L from the back of the car-park in the direction of an immediately visible upright bondstone. Continue over the brow of the hill and here there are several small disused granite quarries. Bear R here along a path which then skirts close to the road and continues up the south side of the brooding Lower Man. Keeping Lower Man to the L, turn L between the two bosses of the Tor *(1)* and then go half R to pick up a clear path leading down to the fenced-in Haytor Quarries. On reaching a track (before a solitary granite post and three weather-battered Scots Pine trees) go L to the workings. Go through a gate on the perimeter fence and turn L to explore the quarry and its ponds *(2)*. Retrace your steps to the gate, then go L following the perimeter fence and spoil down and, at the bottom of the slope, go L to pick up the granite tramway. Stretches of the tramway have become severely eroded and chestnut paling draws attention to those areas being restored; walk parallel to the tramway to help the recovery process. Follow the tramway, passing a set of granite points, until reaching a junction between this branch line and the main line to Holwell Tor. Turn L at the junction and follow the tramway through a shallow cutting and down to its terminal beyond the

Following page: Crane winding gear, Haytor Quarries.

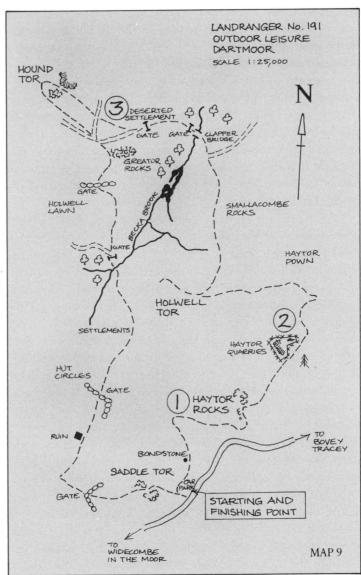

LANDRANGER No. 191
OUTDOOR LEISURE
DARTMOOR
SCALE 1:25,000

MAP 9

sheer worked face of Holwell Quarry. Retrace your steps back up the tramway passing a level spoil area on the L, a ruined building on the R and a set of granite points; keep on the L fork, and by the next set of points—near several small rowan trees—take the narrow path on the L which leads to the summit of Smallacombe Rocks. Views here of the Becka Brook valley are outstanding. Continue straight on over the summit and then bear half L on a path which leads to the valley bottom. On the way down this path unites with a public bridlepath (coming in on the R). Continue straight on here (PBS 'to Houndtor'). The path now enters the valley bottom woods where alder, blackthorn, rowan, hawthorn, birch and oak grow in wild profusion and natural confusion.

Cross over the clapper bridge at the Becka Brook and continue straight on up the steep valley side passing through a wooden gate. At the top of the hill Greator Rocks are close by on the L. The path here continues straight on down to the pre-Conquest settlement site of Houndtor *(3)*. From the village go straight on to Hound Tor, a massive tor steeped in superstition and legend. On reaching the summit, go through the central avenue of the tor and then bear half back L. Make for the R side of Greator Rocks, passing through a gap in the low banks of former field boundaries and keeping the settlement site down on the L.

Keeping the tor on the L (although it is well worth a slight detour here to explore these rocks) continue half R following a small path which leads to a wider track to a gateway in the enclosure wall ahead. The gateway carries a small information board and a fingerpost. On reaching the gate, the information board draws attention to the Agreement made between the landowner and the National Park Authority which allows access, along defined paths, through Holwell Lawn. A smaller sign here informs us that 'There may be a bull in this area at certain times. He will be a beef bull, running with cows or heifers, and in these circumstances is considered not to be dangerous.' Having being thus reassured, go through the gate and turn L onto a path waymarked 'Haytor Down'. At the next waymark post turn L downslope, again waymarked 'Haytor Down'. Go through the small wooden gate and follow the path to the R through the trees to the Becka Brook. Cross the infant river and go on up-slope to a path running parallel with the valley. Here, turn R and follow the path through the bracken. After several hundred yards it is necessary to go half L up to the clitter slope, below several outcrops, to avoid very boggy ground; drier ground here through the bracken allows easier passage up the valley. Continue round (L) the clitter slope and, with Rippon Tor in view ahead, make for the enclosure wall. The wall does a slight 'dog leg' to the L and here is a gate with another small access agreement information board. This agreement allows access, again on defined paths, through the Emsworthy enclosures. Go through the gate (waymarked 'Footpath to Common nr Hemsworthy Gate') and continue straight on along the path (waymarked red) passing the tumbled-down walls and field ruins of Emsworthy on the R. Turn L at next path junction (waymarked 'To Saddle Tor') and leave the Emsworthy enclosures via a gate. Continue half L for the summit of Saddle Tor and drop down to the car-park.

Previous page: *Hound Tor.*

Above: *Hound Tor, with Hay Tor in the distance.*

1 *Haytor Down and Haytor Rocks*

Haytor Down and Haytor Rocks, an area of 1089 acres (441 ha) was bought by the Dartmoor National Park Authority (Devon County Council) in 1975 to help protect the area from the consequences of its own popularity. The tor itself has been popular with the people of Devon for over a century and it now attracts many thousands of visitors each year.

2 *Haytor Quarries*

The Haytor Granite Quarries were leased from the Duke of Somerset by the Templer Family. James Templer had made his fortune in India and established a country seat in the middle of the eighteenth century at nearby Stover. He built Stover Canal, completed in about 1800, to exploit the great deposits of ball clay in the Teign valley. Even at this time the excellence of Haytor granite for building purposes was recognized.

3 *Houndtor*

Houndtor deserted settlement today comprises the substantial remains of a cluster of buildings—four dwellings and their ancillary structures—and an outlying farmstead a short distance to the north west. The whole settlement is surrounded by prehistoric enclosures.

2.8

Cox Tor—White Tor—Staple Tors

STARTING AND FINISHING POINT

Large car-park on the B3357 at the top of Pork Hill, 3 miles east of Tavistock; 1½ miles (2.5 km) west of Merrivale (191-531751).

LENGTH

7½ miles (12.25 km)

ASCENT

One climb: ¾ mile (1.2 km), ascent 384 ft (117 m) to Cox Tor summit; and three climbs of ⅓ mile (0.5 km) in length; ascent 382 ft (100 m) to Smeardon Down; 289 ft (88 m) to White Tor; and 112 ft (34 m) to Roos Tor.

This walk begins by traversing the dramatic, bench-like slopes of Cox Tor. A prehistoric stone row, standing stone and stone circle and an eighteenth-century suicide's grave add further human dimension to this imposing landscape.

The walk enters the Merrivale Firing Range from White Tor to Roos Tor. Firing times will need to be checked.

ROUTE DESCRIPTION (Maps 10, 11)

From the middle of the car-park cross over the road and head for the summit of Cox Tor (*1*) keeping a spring and wet flush area on the L. At the head of the spring bear half L and begin to zig-zag to the summit. Continue over the crest of the tor passing a prehistoric stone cairn and go straight on. With Higher Godsworthy directly ahead go half L down the slope tacking round the clitter slope to the road. Cross the road and by the corner of a large field go through the gate (PBS). Follow the edge of this field (boundary on the R) and enter another field which contains a large outcrop on the L. Soon the bridlepath divides; take the right fork and follow through the field of rough grazing, until the far north western corner. Here go through the gate, go R and follow the walled track down to Great Combe Tor.

From the tor go half R and follow the boundary wall down to the Colly Brook. At the brook bear L and follow downstream passing a series of small, and several large, waterfalls. At the lowest, largest fall follow the path which leads half L away from the river. Cross over a small leat and pass an artificial pond. Cut down the slope half R and go over the footbridge crossing the Colly Brook. Ignoring the paths to L and R continue straight on up slope and, at the cottage, go L through a gate and follow this track to the lane.

Cross the lane and tack up, half R, to the summit of Smeardon Down. Go R along the crest and pass Boulters Tor

Following page: In Peter Tavy Combe.

65

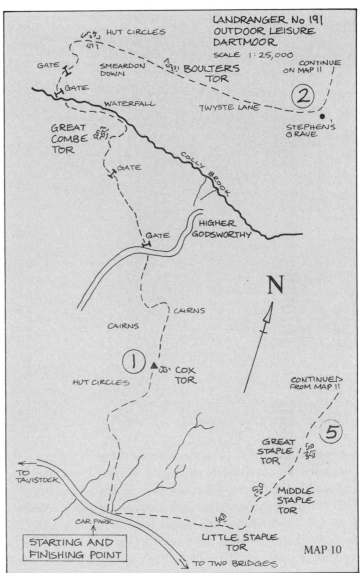

(L), where tor and stone walling appear as one. Continue along the clearly-defined, walled peat track (Twyste Lane) which separates the enclosures ahead. On reaching the open moor continue along the track to Stephen's Grave (R) *(2)*.

At the grave go L and follow the bridlepath keeping stone walls on L. Before the wall bends away half L turn R and go up-slope, passing a prehistoric enclosed settlement and the outcrop of Lower White Tor; then make for White Tor *(3)*, a riot of clitter, crags and the coursing of an Iron Age hill fort. Continue along the summit and head in the same direction to the 'Long Stone' Standing Stone, on Langstone Moor *(4)*. From this menhir follow the stone row to its northern end and retrace

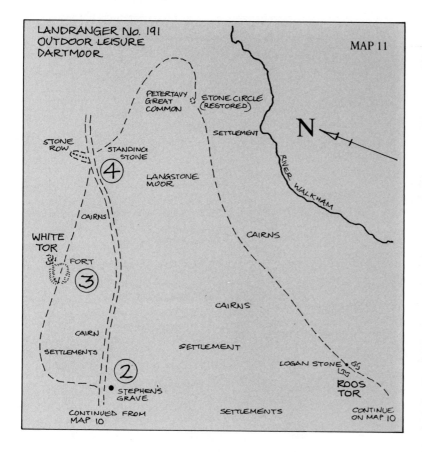

your steps back. With your back to the stone row ignore the peat track and go half L along a path skirting Langstone Mire and head for Langstone Moor Stone Circle flanked by Great Mis Tor. From the stone circle, with this tor on the L, continue along the slowly-rising ridge ahead for Roos Tor, keeping the River Walkham down on the L and keeping above a prehistoric settlement group on the valleyside. From Roos Tor, which is surrounded by a ring of bond stones, the torscape of the Walkham Valley is spectacular.

Continue on in the same direction for Great Staple Tor. Rock basins, vast clitter slopes and an avenue between the remnant stacks—this is one of Dartmoor's greatest tors (5). Continue on down to Middle Staple Tor and thence continue straight on keeping to the L of Little Staple Tor for an exploration of the abundant worked stone in this area. Cut right to Little Staple Tor and then continue on downslope towards the road crossing over the extensive tin working gulleys. Follow the road for the return to the car-park.

1 Cox Tor

During the Quaternary period, which began some 1.7 million

Previous page: *View west from Boulter's Tor, showing Peter Tavy Church (left) and Mary Tavy Church (right).*

years ago, there have been at least 17 cold phases during which most of the British Isles was affected by the repeated advance and retreat of vast ice sheets. These ice sheets from the north reached Devon only once, but the cliffs of Bideford Bay halted the southern advance of that ice sheet and Dartmoor, therefore, escaped glaciation. However, it has been affected by a variety of cold-climate weathering and erosion processes during these phases, processes which subtly still go on today.

Frost shattering and riving of exposed bedrock, together with the subsequent downslope transfer of material has resulted in marked benches (so-called cryoplanation or antiplanation terraces) on some Dartmoor slopes. Cox Tor reveals a staircase of at least five such terraces, the metamorphic (altered) rocks here being particularly susceptible to this process. Similar forces have been at work on Smeardon Down and White Tor.

2 Stephen's Grave

At Stephen's Grave a simple stone is a memorial to John Stephen whose death occurred in October 1762. He was a young man of Peter Tavy who was driven to take his own life by the unfaithfulness of the girl to whom he was betrothed. His ghost was said to haunt the area, which disturbed the inhabitants of Peter Tavy so much that the parson was asked to lay the ghost; this he did on a night when a terrible storm was raging. For many years the stone pillar was leaning and insecure until it was set up on a plinth by the Dartmoor Preservation Association in May 1936.

3 White Tor

White Tor is a prehistoric fortified stronghold, dating from the Iron Age, and its siting around a tor is unique. A double line of stone ramparts encircle the tor and in many places, especially on the east side, outcrops of rock are incorporated in them. These ramparts enclose about 1½ acres (0.6 ha). The fort appears to have been a place of refuge in times of danger rather than being permanently occupied. On the south west slope of the tor are two oval shelters and at the west end another; these may have been shepherds' shelters.

4 The Stones of Langstone Moor

At the head of Langstone Moor mire is a dispersed collection of prehistoric monuments including a standing stone, a stone row and a stone circle. The menhir, known as the 'Long Stone', stands 9 feet (2.7 m) above the ground and is the southern terminal stone to a ruined stone row—some 110 yards (101 m) long—which was discovered in 1893. A few hundred yards away to the south east is the Langstone Moor

Approaching Langstone Moor along Twyste Lane.

Stone Circle. This impressively-sited circle, also known as the 'Ring-of-Stones', was re-erected towards the end of the last century and it then comprised sixteen stones. During World War II the monument was severely damaged by troops training on the moor. Today, only six stones stand to their full height, four are fallen and broken and six are stumps with their heads deliberately knocked off and laying on the ground nearby. The Long Stone too was used for target practice—the marks of gunfire are visible on it. All these monuments are of epidiorite, an altered igneous rock, and not of granite like most Dartmoor prehistoric remains.

5 *Great Staple Tor*

Great Staple Tor consists of remnant stacks on either side of a natural avenue, these piles being described as 'steeples' and likened to the Colossi.

The rocks here assume fantastic shapes and some are precariously poised. 'Staple Tor Tolmen' comprises a pile of four huge granite blocks. Tolmens are stones with holes in them and as such were thought to possess magical properties.

THE HIGHEST LAND IN SOUTHERN ENGLAND

STARTING AND FINISHING POINT
Meldon Reservoir, (191-562917) situated approximately 3 miles (5 km) to the south west of Okehampton, highway signposted from the A30. Construction of the controversial Okehampton Bypass began in November 1986; the road is due for completion in December 1988 and involves the building of a new slip road to Meldon. Park in the large car-park on L approaching the reservoir.
LENGTH
6.5 miles (10 km)
ASCENT
One climb: 2 miles (3 km), ascent 1145 ft (349 m) to Yes Tor.

The walk crosses Meldon dam and follows the West Okement downstream to an area of considerable interest for its industrial archaeology and for its geology. It follows the beautiful Red-a-ven Brook upstream to the lower slopes of Yes Tor and then crosses Dartmoor's highest land to the timeless outcrop of Black Tor.

This walk must not be attempted in poor weather—visibility on the moors can fall rapidly and it may be difficult to find your way back. The walk also enters the Okehampton Firing Range; firing times must be checked.

ROUTE DESCRIPTION (Map 12)

From the landscaped car-park and picnic area, owned by the National Park Authority, pass the toilet block (information board here) and go through the gate. Turn L and follow the lane to the dam (PBS 'Bridlepath to the moor'). Cross over the massive concrete dam *(1)* which impounds the steep-sided valley of the West Okement River. From the dam are dramatic views over the reservoir where Homerton Hill drops beneath the water's edge on its south eastern side. Downstream can be seen the currently worked British Rail's Meldon Quarry (which supplies some 2000 tons of ballast a day), as well as smaller abandoned ones; the massive iron structure of the now unused Meldon viaduct provides an imposing backdrop. Go through the gates at the far end of the dam and turn immediately L through another gate; follow the steps down to the base of the dam.

Walk downstream from the dam on the river's R bank. Cross over the Red-a-ven Brook near to its confluence with the West Okement River. After the Brook carry on straight ahead; do not follow the track round to the R. After some 50 yards (45 m) turn L to cross over the long narrow wooden footbridge which spans the West Okement; a drowned limestone quarry lies opposite *(2)*. Retrace your steps over the bridge and go L along a

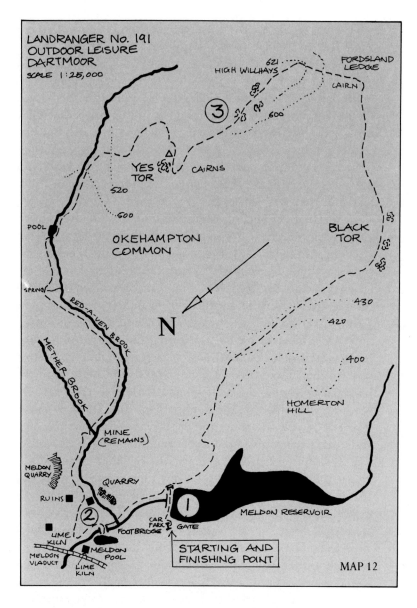

LANDRANGER No. 191
OUTDOOR LEISURE
DARTMOOR
SCALE 1:25,000

FORDSLAND
LEDGE
HIGH WILLHAYS 621
CAIRN
③
600
YES TOR
CAIRNS
520
500
POOL
OKEHAMPTON
COMMON
BLACK TOR
SPRING
RED-A-VEN BROOK
N
430
420
METHER BROOK
400
MINE
(REMAINS)
HOMERTON
HILL
MELDON
QUARRY
RUINS
QUARRY
②
CAR PARK
GATE
FOOTBRIDGE
MELDON RESERVOIR
LIME KILN
MELDON
VIADUCT
MELDON
POOL
LIME
KILN

STARTING AND
FINISHING POINT

MAP 12

path skirting the edge of the partially grassed-over spoil heaps
(on R). Keeping the river on the L, follow the track down
towards the viaduct passing a small disused building on the L.
Stop by the telegraph pole and ahead lies the restored remains
of a large lime kiln—well worth a visit. Retrace steps to the
telegraph pole and follow the path round (half L) and head for
the large and gaping disused quarry. Keep this quarry on the
opposite side of the Red-a-ven Brook; go up the valley passing a
massive walled structure and just beyond a smaller non-working
quarry on the L.

Follow the track upstream, with the river to the R, passing
numerous small waterfalls and pools. At the Range Noticeboard

walk down to the river (on R). Here are the remains of an old mine. Return upslope to the Noticeboard and cross the stream (the Mether Brook) and continue straight on keeping two small isolated hawthorn trees to the L. Where a very steep-sided valley known as Sniper's Gully (on R) joins the Red-a-ven Brook, follow the Red-a-ven round to the L. Soon the valley closes in on us. The path becomes ill-defined in places but stay close to the river. The valley soon opens out and a stream issues from a spring ahead, upslope on the L. Turn half L to skirt above the spring, to avoid very boggy ground, and then continue half R to rejoin the riverbank near Yes Tor Ford. Do not cross the river here but continue upstream heading for a series of falls.

The valley begins to get much steeper. Keep the large gully of a redundant military target railway on your L and climb to the small dam and overspill which impound the Red-a-ven Brook forming a small, but deep, pool. This was constructed before the turn of the century to augment Okehampton's water supply. Taking care, we need to cross the river here. Go on upstream, now with the river on the L. Nearing the river's source, the Red-a-ven Brook becomes more of a stream although during wet weather it can become quite violent. The route from the pool can be boggy; the drier ground is close to the river. On reaching a low bluff on the R, after West Mill Tor is to three-quarters L, go R and above the bluff for Yes Tor summit; on a clear day a Range mast and OS Triangulation Point are visible. The route to the Tor encounters a massive clitter slope and it is best to avoid a scramble by following round to the L to ascend the final leg to the Tor's summit. The Tor is worthy of exploration; a ruined prehistoric stone cairn lies on its north-west side. An OS Triangulation Point and the unfortunately-sited military paraphernalia of lookout hut, stable and range pole (although a potentially useful guide if caught in a mist here as the wires rattle in a wind) and wide, heavily-eroded tracks distort a sense of wilderness, unless the soul and mind can overlook such things. The views are extensive—east Cornwall, north and east Devon and Somerset, and much of the northern moors of Dartmoor can be panned.

Walk straight along (due south) the ridge top to the much smaller outcrops—in size, but not height above sea level—of High Willhays (3). Standing on the top of the southernmost pile which terminates the ridge top look to three-quarters R in the direction of the distant, brooding, Great Links Tor; head along a track to the military lookout hut and stable on Fordsland Ledge. Much of Dartmoor's wildest scenery lies before us. Turn R at the lookout hut and pass a prehistoric cairn. Continue in the same direction, bearing slightly to the L, and head down the

Meldon Reservoir.

grass and heather slope to the three granite piles comprising Black Tor.

Aim for the first (southernmost) pile. Keep to the little-used paths, passing a Range Noticeboard on approach, to avoid boggy ground. Continue straight on—to the middle pile with its extensive clitter slopes. Make for the final outcrop and continue half R for an obvious unmetalled vehicle track running over Longstone Hill. Go along this track until Meldon Reservoir comes into view and cut down the slope (half L) for the dam and car-park.

1 *Meldon Reservoir*

The West Okement Valley has been dramatically plugged by the creation of Meldon Reservoir. First mooted in 1962 the consultation process proved to be a long drawn-out saga with the National Park Committee and local and national amenity societies fighting to save what was without doubt an outstanding valley.

The dam is 660 feet (201 m) long and 144 feet (44 m) high and cost £1.6 million to build. The reservoir thus created covers an area of 57 acres (23 ha), its maximum depth of water is 132 feet (40 m) and it has a maximum capacity of 680 million gallons (over 3000 million litres). Water from here is supplied to a population of 200,000 in an area extending from Tavistock in the south to Bideford in the north.

2 *Meldon Pool*

The geology of the Meldon area is extremely complex and

superimposed onto this is a confusing history of past industrial activity which exploited the rock and mineral resources found.

Meldon Pool is 130 feet (40 m) deep and occupies an old limestone quarry. The limited outcrops of limestone in the area were important for producing lime for agricultural purposes in the eighteenth and nineteenth centuries. Near the pool are two limekilns and the one on the river's right

Up the Red-a-ven Brook, with Yes Tor on the right.

bank was consolidated by the National Park Authority in 1984; this kiln dates from the eighteenth century and is one of the oldest known on Dartmoor.

3 High Willhays

At some 2038 ft (621 m) above sea level, High Willhays is the highest land in England south of Kinder Scout (2088 ft, 636 m) in the Peak District, some 250 miles (402 km) away.

NORSWORTHY BRIDGE—EYLESBARROW —DITSWORTHY WARREN— SHEEPSTOR

Norsworthy Bridge at north east end of Burrator Reservoir (202-568693). Take B3212 Yelverton to Princetown road and at Dousland, on approach from Yelverton, go R following highway signs for Burrator and Sheepstor. At Burrator Dam continue straight on for 1½ miles (2.5 km) to Norsworthy Bridge. Car-parking area here on both sides of the road beyond the bridge, 10 miles (16 km) due north west of Plymouth.

LENGTH
7½ miles (12 km)

ASCENT
Three climbs: ⅓ mile (0.6 km), ascent 341 ft (104 m) to Down Tor; ¾ mile (1.2 km), ascent 259 ft (79 m) to Eylesbarrow; ½ mile (0.75 km), ascent 233 ft (71 m) to Sheeps Tor summit.

This area of south west Dartmoor contains some of the National Park's most beautiful scenery and is dominated by the huge pile of Sheeps Tor. South-west Dartmoor also contains a rich variety of antiquities embraced by these wild settings. Included on the route are the remains of our past, spanning some 3500 years. The route also passes Ditsworthy Warren—a commercial rabbit warren which closed in the mid-1950s.

ROUTE DESCRIPTION (Maps 13, 14)

With Norsworthy Bridge, spanning the River Meavy, on the L continue along the road in the direction of Sheepstor going over the small road bridge which crosses the Narrator Brook. Within a few yards the road begins to bear half R. Here, leave the road and continue straight ahead along the walled lane (with forest edge on the R). Pass the remains of Middleworth Farm on the R *(1)*; Middleworth Tor can be seen rising above the trees on the L. On reaching the ruins of the farm settlement at Deancombe, pass the first group of buildings which date from medieval times and before reaching the nineteenth-century remains go L up a rugged tree-lined path, next to an old mine adit. Continue on up passing a sheep pen and go through a gate directly ahead which leads onto the open moor. Follow the path straight up for a short distance, then bear half L for the summit of Down Tor.

From Down Tor go R through the clitter field on the eastern slope and make for a path running parallel with, and to the L of,

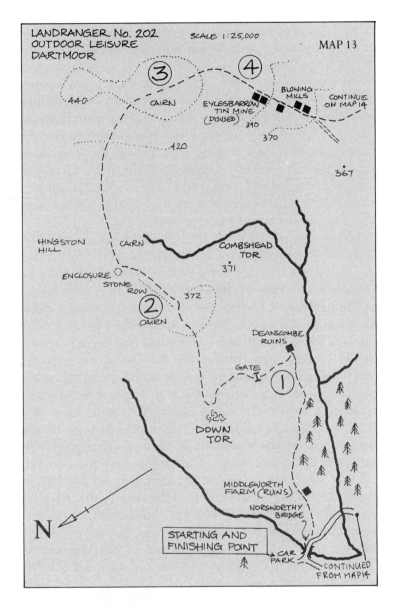

LANDRANGER No. 202
OUTDOOR LEISURE
DARTMOOR

SCALE 1:25,000

MAP 13

the large stone-walled enclosure. Follow the path uphill and where the wall bends away to the R continue half L through the clitter to the crest of this hill. Cross the low banked boundary work (a prehistoric reave) near a cairn and head for the retaining circle and single stone row on the level plain of Hingston Hill (2). Follow the row to the furthest end and continue half L for a circular enclosure and from here go straight on to the cairn, a massive heap of stones. From the cairn continue straight on, keeping the tinners' gullies on the R. At the head of these workings go half R and ascend the hill to the summit of Eylesbarrow (3).

At the PCWW 1917 bondstone, situated between two

prehistoric cairns, continue straight on along a path which drops down to the ruins of Eylesbarrow Tin Mine *(4)* in the direction of the distant china clay spoil heaps.

On approach bear half L and head for the furthest building backdropped by Higher Hartor Tor. Some shafts at Eylesbarrow are only partly filled in and care should be taken when exploring the area. Turn R onto the track and follow down passing the foundations of former blowing mills and on the R a line of granite flat-rod supports. Continue on the track passing an isolated substantial wall, being part of a blowing mill, L and after some 200 yards (219 m) another track leads off to half L. Follow this down to the ruined smelting house.

Follow this track beyond the smelting house to the ford, cross over the Drizzlecombe and contour round to the R in the direction of the hillside outcrop of Shavercombe Tor. Make for Drizzlecombe prehistoric stone rows and the huge cairn known as Giant's Basin *(5)*. Follow the rows down to the last menhir. Continue on in the same direction heading for a group of Scots Pine on the skyline to the L of Eastern Tor to pick a track leading to Ditsworthy Warren *(6)*. Pass the kennel enclosure and house (L) at Ditsworthy Warren and, noticing the pillow mounds ahead, bear immediately R to follow Edward's Path contouring the lower slopes of Eastern Tor; keep Gutter Mire down to the L. On reaching a clump of pine trees go through the gate, passing the Scouts Hut on the R. Go through another gate and turn R onto the track and follow for some 150 yards (137 m). After crossing the leat go L and follow the line, but not the bank so as to prevent erosion, of this watercourse. Keep the leat on the L until two PCWW 1917 bondstones are reached. Here, cross over the leat L, picking the spot that will not disturb the leat banks. Continue straight on, in the direction of Yellowmead Farm. On approaching the enclosure wall bear half R to Yellowmead Stone Circle *(7)*.

The leat further on from here is too wide to cross and it is necessary to retrace steps back to the bondstones. Cross the leat once more and bear L to follow the leat uphill. Where the leat swings abruptly to the L, continue half L to the summit of Sheeps Tor *(8)*. Follow the summit ridge northwards (L) then bear R back down the slope and, half way down, go left heading for Narrator Plantation. Follow the beech-topped wall to the L down to a hunt gate. Go through the gate and on the R are the ruins of Narrator Farm, evacuated and demolished after the building of Burrator Reservoir. Follow the bridlepath half L, between two granite gateposts and on reaching the road go R and follow for about ½ mile (0.8 km) to return to Norsworthy Bridge.

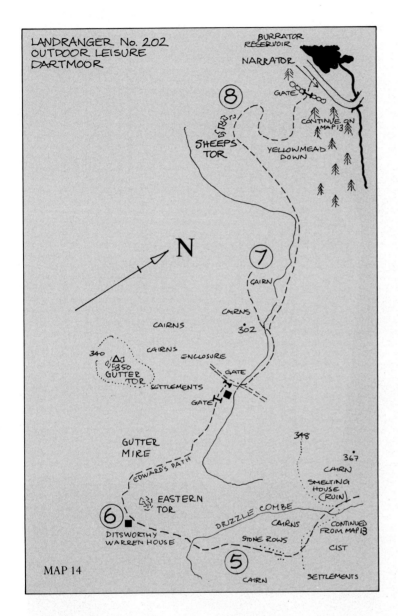

1 Abandoned farms

Middleworth, Deancombe and Narrator farms, along with about eight others, were evacuated and demolished sometime following the completion of the Burrator Reservoir in 1895 and before its subsequent enlargement in 1928. At Middleworth the dwelling house has almost disappeared following the farm's abandonment in about 1915 after a history of some 634 years. A fine barn survives to its full height, having an upper floor, though roofless, and bears a date-stone—'ML 1885'—in the top left hand corner of the outside west wall; the initials 'ML' refer to the landowner at that time—Manasseh Lopes.

2 *Hingston Hill*

The prehistoric monuments on Hingston Hill (Down Tor) are evocatively sited. Here a retaining circle measures some 37 feet (11.2 m) across and this entirely encloses a cairn in which a kistvaen, now gone, was centrally placed. Running eastward from this circle and beginning with a stone almost 10 feet (3 m) high is a single stone row—1145 feet (349 m) in length and which terminates at a blockingstone. Just beyond its eastern end is a large stone cairn and to the north-west of this is a large pound. The standing stones which had fallen down were set back up again in the summer of 1894.

3 *Eylesbarrow*

The great dome of Eylesbarrow rises to 1489 feet (454 m) above sea level and the views from it are very extensive and take in much of the blanket bog areas of the south and north moors.

4 *Eylesbarrow Tin Mine*

The remains of Eylesbarrow Tin Mine lie to the north of the River Plym, some 2 miles (3.2 km) from the river's source. Tinners were known to be streaming in the area in the twelfth century and the earliest known mining reference to Eylesbarrow is 1671.

5 *Drizzlecombe and the Giant's Basin*

Certain places on Dartmoor acquired a special sanctity amongst prehistoric peoples and sometime around 2500 BC they were putting up standing stones often associated with small cairns containing stone coffins or kistvaens. Taken as a whole, the prehistoric remains at Drizzlecombe are amongst the finest on Dartmoor. Here three parallel rows are each headed by a ruined grave with a retaining circle and terminated by a large menhir. The south-east menhir stands 14 feet (4 m) high and is the tallest on Dartmoor.

Close to the rows is a massive cairn, known as the Giant's Basin, a great heap of stones, hollowed out, with a diameter of 70 feet (21.3 m). Whether this large burial barrow is contemporary with the rows has not, as yet, been ascertained. Barrows of this size are usually of a later period, somewhere around 2000 BC. Likewise, the settlement groups to the north-east of the rows may be of a later period.

6 *Ditsworthy Warren*

The Norman Conquest in 1066 brought with it the introduction of the rabbit. These soon became a useful source of food and purpose-built warrens arose in many parts of the country including nineteen on Dartmoor. The oldest on Dartmoor was Trowlesworthy in the Plym valley and dates from the thirteenth century. The medieval-founded Dits-

Opposite: *Menhir, Drizzlecombe—the largest standing stone on Dartmoor.*

Ditsworthy Warren House.

worthy Warren originally extended for 230 acres (93 ha) but was enlarged to cover 1100 acres (445 ha) to form the largest of the Dartmoor warrens.

7 *Yellowmead Stone Circle*

Yellowmead prehistoric multiple stone circle dates from the third millenium BC. It was discovered in 1921 after drought conditions indicated buried stones in an area where dense heather had recently been burnt. The fallen stones were uncovered and erected where they lay later that year. The circle has four concentric rings with diameters of about 21, 38, 48 and 65 feet (6.4, 11.6, 14.6 and 20 m).

8 *Sheeps Tor*

The views to and from the massive granite mass of Sheeps Tor are outstanding. On its summit, within the clitter, is the Pixies' Cave—a natural formation which if you discover you should leave a pin or some other offering for good luck. The cave, it is said, offered refuge for a local eminent Royalist during the Civil War.

3.11

BELSTONE—STEEPERTON TOR—COSDON HILL

STARTING AND FINISHING POINT

Belstone village, which lies to the south of the old A30 running through Sticklepath; 3 miles (5 km) south east of Okehampton, 5 miles (8 km) west of Whiddon Down (191-619936).

LENGTH

10 miles (16 km)

ASCENT

4 climbs: ¼ mile (1.2 km), ascent 328 ft (100 m) to Belstone Tor; ½ mile (0.75 km), ascent 270 ft (82 m) to Steeperton Tor; 1¼ miles (2 km), ascent 262 ft (80 m) to Cosdon Hill; ⅛ mile (0.5 km), ascent 121 ft (37 m) from River Taw to Belstone village.

This walk ventures into some of Dartmoor's wildest moorland and it should not be attempted in poor weather. The southern portion of this walk (from Knattaborough to Steeperton Tor) is within the Okehampton Firing Range; check the firing programme before setting out.

ROUTE DESCRIPTION (Maps 15, 16)

From the centre of the village (1), keeping the Tors Inn and the Old Barton on the L and the Old Post Office ('Telegraph Office') on the R take the L fork just uphill, ignoring the first turning on the L which leads to the church. The lane is signed 'Dartmoor. No through road'. Pass the Belstone Treatment Works (on R) and continue on to the moorgate at Watchet. Go through the gate and continue straight on along the track, keeping the stone wall close to the R. Where the track divides, near to where the wall bends away to the R, take the L fork and after about 50 yards (46 m) go half L to the Nine Maidens prehistoric stone circle (2).

Go straight on following a grassy path up to Tors End, the northernmost outcrop on Watchet Hill which marks the beginning of the Belstone range of tors. Go round the L side (east) of the tor; here there is much evidence of the stone cutter's presence. From Tors End continue straight on up to the next outcrop; keep on the path to the R for this tor. Go straight on along the ridge crest and skirting the L side of Belstone Tor go straight on over the Irishman's Wall (3) and then to Higher Tor where rowan, bilberry and tenuous moorland grasses seemingly grow out of the granite.

From Higher Tor go down slope to two upright boundary stones on the ridge crest, then head slightly to the R and pass a small grass-covered prehistoric cairn. Continue along the ridge to the next outcrop, known as Knattaborough. At this point you enter the Okehampton Firing Range.

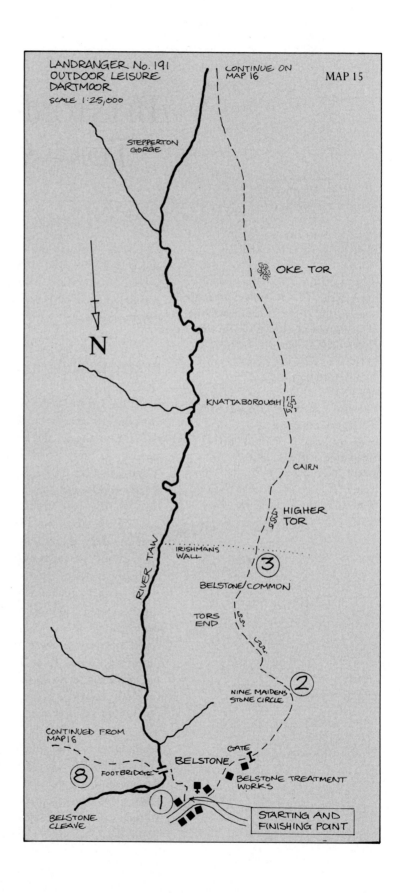

LANDRANGER No. 191
OUTDOOR LEISURE
DARTMOOR
SCALE 1:25,000

CONTINUE ON
MAP 16

MAP 15

STEPPERTON
GORGE

N

OKE TOR

KNATTABOROUGH

CAIRN

HIGHER
TOR

IRISHMANS
WALL

③

BELSTONE COMMON

TORS
END

②

NINE MAIDENS
STONE CIRCLE

RIVER TAW

CONTINUED FROM
MAP 16

⑧   FOOTBRIDGE

BELSTONE

GATE

BELSTONE TREATMENT
WORKS

①

BELSTONE
CLEAVE

STARTING AND
FINISHING POINT

A natural death—Belstone Common.

If you should hear firing when in a no-firing period this will be military dry-training practice which involves no live ammunition and although disconcerting it is safe to proceed. Follow the grass track to Oke Tor for extensive views over highest Dartmoor to the west; High Willhays at 2038 feet (621 m), Dartmoor's highest point actually looks lower than its neighbour Yes Tor (2031 feet, 619 m). The penetration of the northern moor by military roads and tracks clearly visible from here is an unfortunate intrusion in this wilderness. Keeping the military look-out and stable huts, on the southern end of the Tor, on the R, continue straight on along the track to a ford over the River Taw. Here, keeping the river on the L, follow a small path upstream for about 150 yards (137 m) to the remains of Knack Mine, a small nineteenth-century tin venture. Retrace steps to the ford and cross over the river noticing the remains of a clapper bridge here.

Continue on the track upstream for a few yards then take the steep path on the L which leads up to Steeperton Tor *(4)*; aim for the look-out hut. From the hut go R and, on reaching the southernmost outcrop take the small path on ½ L which leads in the direction of Wild Tor. This path peters out in places, but continue on down to a ford over the Steeperton Brook; the approach can be very boggy. Keep on the L bank of the river and follow downstream for 50 yards (46 m) to the ruins of a medieval tinners' house. Retrace your steps to the ford, cross over the river and, just up slope ahead, go L down a well-defined track (often very wet on some stretches). Continue on the path passing Hound Tor on the R and where the track divides go R to the White Moor Stone Circle *(5)*. Here too is an

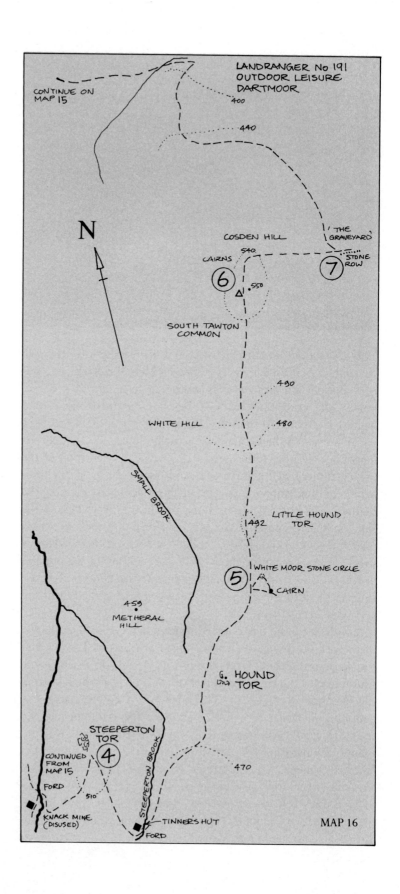

LANDRANGER No 191
OUTDOOR LEISURE
DARTMOOR

400

440

CONTINUE ON
MAP 15

N

THE
GRAVEYARD

COSDEN HILL

CAIRNS

540

STONE
ROW

⑥

.550
△

⑦

SOUTH TAWTON
COMMON

490

WHITE HILL

.480

SMALL BROOK

LITTLE HOUND
TOR

1492

⑤ | WHITE MOOR STONE CIRCLE
CAIRN

459
.
METHERAL
HILL

G. HOUND
TOR

STEEPERTON
TOR
④

CONTINUED
FROM
MAP 15

STEEPERTON BROOK

470

FORD

510

KNACK MINE
(DISUSED)

TINNER'S HUT
FORD

MAP 16

upright bondstone and a prehistoric cairn. Retrace your steps back to where the track divides and, ignoring the bridlepath to the L and R, follow the path which leads over the low rise of Little Hound Tor and continue straight on uphill to the cairn-topped summit of Cosdon Hill *(6)*.

Continue along the ridge to the furthest (northernmost) cairn. Go R here downslope; Castle Drogo lies straight ahead (due east) some 5½ miles (9 km) away. The path down becomes hard to follow and the going through bilberry, bracken and heather can be rough in places. Where the steep slope begins to level out aim for the prehistoric triple stone row near the head of Cheriton Combe on the R *(7)*.

From the nearest end of the stone row bear half L upslope through an extensive area of bracken and begin to contour round the north east side of Cosdon Hill. Keep well to the L of an isolated bondstone on South Zeal Common near Foxes' Holt. On reaching the well-used bridlepath, which leads to Cosdon Beacon from the north side of the hill, turn R and follow down to its junction with another bridlepath. Turn L and continue

Above: A military track on Belstone Common.

Following page: 'The Graveyard', triple stone row, Cosdon Hill.

straight on over the channel of a disused leat and head for Belstone keeping Belstone Cleave well down on R. The views here to Belstone and over the Cleave to mid-Devon and beyond are outstanding *(8)*. A path drops down to the bottom of the Taw Valley below Belstone village; cross over the footbridge here and continue on the path up the valleyside to return to the village.

1 *Belstone village*

The small village of Belstone is worthy of exploration. The old stocks still stand on the village green and nearby is a small pound in which stray animals were impounded. The village Post Office, which has a name-stone denoting it as the 'Telegraph Office', was once a Zion Chapel—a datestone of 1841 can be seen above the front door. The church, dedicated to St. Mary, dates from the fifteenth century and is famed for its peal of six bells, five of which are eighteenth-century while the sixth was added in 1955. By the church gate once stood an almshouse; the old village inn disappeared in 1896.

2 *The Nine Maidens*

The Nine Maidens is a large prehistoric retaining circle. Today it consists of about sixteen stones, but some of the original stones may have been lost to stone masons and time—the circle is also known as the Seventeen Brothers.

In legend these stones were once flesh and blood, being a band of merry maidens who met here to dance upon a Sunday. For partaking in such an act they were turned to stone and compelled to dance every day at noon.

3 *Irishman's Wall*

The broken-down boundary work of the Irishman's Wall is a lasting testimony of the folly of trying to infringe upon the rights of common. One explanation of the wall's origin concerns a band of Irish Protestants who, driven from Ulster in the eighteenth century, attempted a settlement on this part of Dartmoor; here they wanted to create a vast enclosure of moorland for cultivation.

The parishioners of Belstone and Okehampton were, understandably, irate and they destroyed the wall as soon as it was finished and drove the emigrants away. The facts seem to suggest that the wall was built by Irishmen working for a moorland 'improver' and land grabber known as Matthew Crawford with the locals responding in the same way.

4 *Steeperton Tor*

Steeperton Tor has unusually steep slopes for moorland Dartmoor and it rises almost mountain-like above the waters

of the Steeperton Brook on the one side and the River Taw on the other. Taw Marsh and Plain appear as a natural amphitheatre flanked on three sides by moorland ridges and hills. The River Taw pursues a meandering northerly course through the Plain and unlike all other Dartmoor rivers its course is both direct and independent from its source to the sea at Barnstaple Bay in the Bristol Channel.

5 *White Moor Stone Circle*

White Moor Stone Circle with a diameter of 66 feet (20 m) lies on the saddle between White Hill and Little Hound Tor and was restored by the Dartmoor Exploration Committee in the late 1890s. Down the centuries neglect and wilful damage has taken its toll upon this mysterious and evocative monument—turf cutters, rain and cattle had broken up the surface of the ground near the stones increasing the risk of them falling over; cattle rubbing their coats on the stones were, in time, likely to push them over and stone masons no doubt pillaged the monument. Eighteen stones were re-erected; one had its top broken off and three had lost their lower sections. Today, seventeen stones remain standing.

6 *Cosdon Hill*

Until the nineteenth century the summit of Cosdon Hill was thought to be the highest point on Dartmoor, its great dome actually rising to 1804 feet (550 m) above sea level; such was the illusion of it rising without intervening ground from the lowland country of mid-Devon. A few Neolithic tools have been found on Dartmoor, including a chipped flint axe from Cosdon Hill.

7 *'The Graveyard' stones*

On the east flank of Cosdon Hill at the head of Cheriton Combe is the remarkable 447-feet (136-m) long triple stone row known as 'The Graveyard' or 'The Cemetery'. A damaged kistvaen and retaining-circle heads the west end of this restored row. The row's orientation is almost due east to west. The monument is bisected by an inter-moorland track running from the village of South Zeal to Hangingstone Hill and the eastern end of the row has been robbed.

8 *Belstone Cleave*

The valley by which the Taw passes out of Dartmoor and falls in the vales of mid-Devon is known as Belstone Cleave, a deep, narrow, wooded cleft through the hills—a rock-strewn, tin-streamed wild place. The fine crag of Ivy Tor juts boldly from the south side. A short distance upstream of the tor are the pits of the Ivy Tor Copper Mine, known to have been working in the 1860s and 70s and between 1905 and 1914.

3.12

DARTMOOR'S NORTH WESTERN EDGE

STARTING AND FINISHING POINT

Prewley Moor (191-547909), 4 miles (6.5 km) south west of Okehampton. Take the A30 from Okehampton then turn L onto the A386 towards Tavistock. After ½ mile (0.8 km) take road on L leading to Prewley treatment works (South West Water). Go over the cattle grid and follow the road up for about 250 yards (229 m). Park on R on the common, not more than 15 yards (14 m) from the road.

LENGTH

13½ miles (22 km)

ASCENT

Four climbs: ½ mile (0.8 km) ascent 351 ft (107 m) to Branscombe's Loaf; ¼ mile (0.3 km) ascent 135 ft (41 m) to Great Links Tor; ⅓ mile (0.5 km) ascent 233 ft (71 m) to Hare Tor; 1½ miles (2.5 km) gradual ascent 361 ft (110 m) to peat railway looping point on Corn Ridge.

This walk includes some of moorland Dartmoor's most dramatic views particularly up the valley of the West Okement River and down into Tavy Cleave. The walk also follows the track bed of a nineteenth-century peatworks railway for some 2 miles (3.5 km).

This is an adventurous walk and it should not be attempted in poor visibility. The route enters the Willsworthy and Okehampton Firing Ranges and firing times will need to be checked.

ROUTE DESCRIPTION (Maps 17, 18)

From parking your vehicle on Prewley Common, walk up the road towards the South West Water treatment works which serve Meldon Reservoir. Where the road bends L by the works entrance follow the boundary wall to the R and continue following the wall round in the direction of Sourton Tors. Where the wall bends and drops to the L continue straight on to pass between two bondstones which are halfway up the hill. At the bondstones bear half R to the pits and banks of the former Sourton Tors Ice Works *(1)*. Keeping Sourton Tors on the R, continue up to the crest of the col between Sourton Tors and Corn Ridge and then bear half L for a steep climb to the summit of Corn Ridge. Cut across to a prehistoric cairn and thence to the 'crown' of the ridge—the solitary rock pile of Branscombe's Loaf *(2)*.

Continue almost half L past the 'tor' to contour round the north-eastern edge of Corn Ridge thus avoiding the extremely boggy head of the Lyd Valley on the R. Aim for the small unnamed, granite outcrop ahead keeping above (to R) of a gully on approach. With the three towering rock piles of Black Tor, and with High Willhays, Yes Tor and the West Okement Valley upstream, in view, contour half R to follow the ridge edge round. Keep the West Okement Valley well down to the L *(3)*.

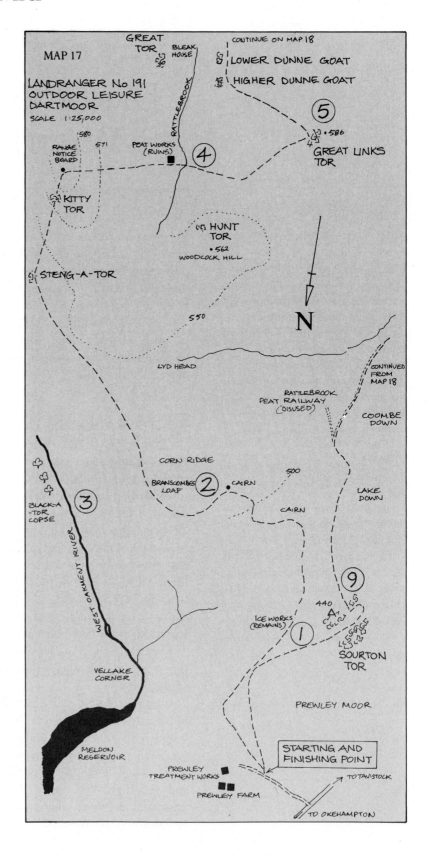

MAP 17

LANDRANGER No 191
OUTDOOR LEISURE
DARTMOOR
SCALE 1:25,000

GREAT
TOR

BLEAK
HOUSE

RATTLEBROOK

CONTINUE ON MAP 18

LOWER DUNNE GOAT

HIGHER DUNNE GOAT

⑤

·580
571

RANGE
NOTICE
BOARD

PEAT WORKS
(RUINS)

④

·586

GREAT LINKS
TOR

KITTY
TOR

HUNT
TOR

·562
WOODCOCK HILL

STENG-A-TOR

550

N

LYD HEAD

RATTLEBROOK
PEAT RAILWAY
(DISUSED)

CONTINUED
FROM
MAP 18

COOMBE
DOWN

CORN RIDGE

BRANSCOMBES
LOAF

②

·CAIRN

500

LAKE
DOWN

BLACK-A
-TOR
COPSE

③

CAIRN

WEST OAKMENT RIVER

⑨

440

ICE WORKS
(REMAINS)

①

SOURTON
TOR

VELLAKE
CORNER

PREWLEY MOOR

STARTING AND
FINISHING POINT

MELDON
RESERVOIR

PREWLEY
TREATMENT WORKS

TO TAVISTOCK

PREWLEY FARM

TO OKEHAMPTON

Bleak House, near Dunna Goat Tors.

Follow a fairly well-defined path, in stretches, to Steng-a-Tor, a small avenue tor. Bad ground lies on the approach and it is necessary to bear half R to avoid this. Keeping R of Okehampton Firing Range boundary poles head half R for Kitty Tor. A path makes its way up over dry ground to the L side of the tor—go to the second range pole to pick up this path. From the lookout hut on this small outcrop go half L for 200 yards (183 m) to a smaller outlying outcrop topped by a Range flag pole.

At the Range Noticeboard, by the flag pole, go half R along a path leading down to the ruined buildings of the Rattlebrook peatworks which are over-shadowed by Great Links Tor. Keep on this path, to avoid boggy ground in and near the artificial drainage channels on the R. The ruined buildings are a scene of utter desolation—brick, granite blockwork, concrete, ironwork and timber baulks lie in a chaotic jumble battered constantly by the very worst of Dartmoor's weather *(4)*.

From the ruins continue in the same direction and go up the track of the old peat railway which runs to the R of Great Links

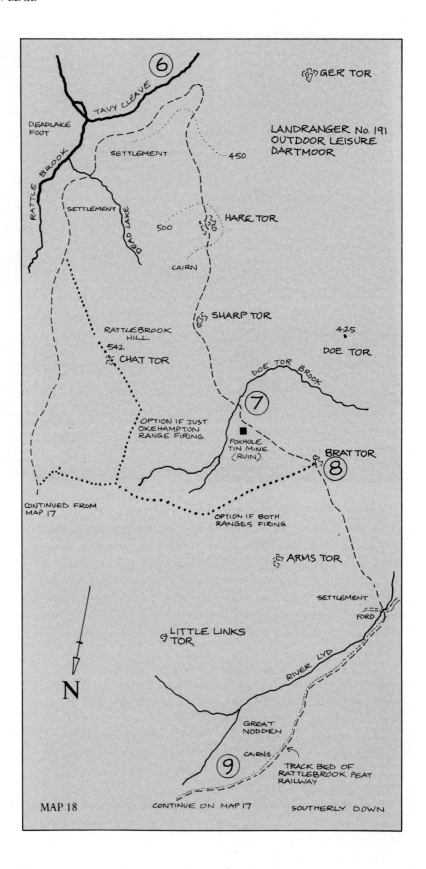

MAP 18

Tor. On reaching the cutting climb up the L side of the track. Great Links Tor comes into view. Follow the track edge for a while and then go L on a small path that leads to the tor *(5)*.

Pass the large free-standing granite pillar on the side of the tor and bear L to the westernmost pile. Turn half R to cut across to the two granite outcrops of Higher and Lower Dunna Goat. At Lower Dunna Goat, after climbing on the summit for extensive views up and downstream the Rattlebrook, keep to the R side of the tor and continue straight on to cross a bridlepath and make your way down (almost half L) to the Rattlebrook valley. If firing on Willsworthy Range is in progress it is possible to omit the southern extension of this walk, to Tavy Cleave, by turning R and taking the bridlepath; at the end of the extensive tin cuttings to the L bear half L following a well-used path to Brat Tor.

If continuing down the Rattlebrook go to Range poles near the valley bottom keeping Chat Tor to half R. From approaching the first pole follow the path which contours around the edge of Rattlebrook Hill skirting well above the flood plain on the L. (If firing is in progress on Okehampton Range only, follow the bridlepath below Lower Dunna Goat to the R towards Dick's Well and go L over Rattlebrook Hill keeping Range poles on the L then go half L for the isolated pile of Chat Tor; keep the tor on the L then cut half R to pick up the path above the Rattlebrook.) With the Green Tor Water and the Scad entering the Rattlebrook immediately opposite, the river begins to meander towards a small gorge as it drops its way down to the Tavy valley. With the upper Tavy valley on the L continue on the path round the side of the hill, half R, whereupon Hare Tor comes into view. Keep the tinning gullies on the L, the path now skirts well to the L of Hare Tor. Aim for a solitary Range Board ('WD Notice: Out of bounds to all troops') and bearing half L here cross the stream of Dead Lake and head almost half L to go over the crest of the spur here close above the edge of Tavy Cleave *(6)*. Ahead lie four unnamed rock piles overlooking the cleave and backdropped in the distance by the pyramidal peak of Ger Tor. On reaching these piles go R to the summit of Hare Tor, at first a gradual but then a much steeper climb.

Continue straight on, northwards, to Sharp Tor. Turn L and make your way downslope, being cautious over the clitter, and aim for a point midway between Brat Tor (with large granite cross) and Arms Tor (to R); on this line on the other side of the Doe Tor Brook head for the ruined buildings amongst the extensive tin workings *(7)*, making your way over the spoil heaps and avoiding wet flushes; bracken denotes the drier ground.

Continue straight on beyond the ruins passing a long walled grass-topped structure—a leat launder—on the R and go to Brat Tor *(8)*. Turn half R from the summit. Head downslope in the direction of the furthest ford, over the River Lyd, which lies to the R of a large enclosure and L of two large river bluffs.

Cross the river and bear half R to cut up the hill. Cross straight over a vehicle track which leads back down to the river, and, on reaching the second track—the bed of the Rattlebrook peat railway—turn R and follow up over the whale-back dome of Great Nodden and over Coombe Down to the railway turning loop on the slopes of Corn Ridge. Go half L, cutting down the hill for 75 yards (68 m) and turn R along a trackway and follow. Where the track forks, bear L and cross the gert, which plunges into Deep Valley. Continue straight on to

Sourton Tors (9). Drop back down to Prewley treatment works (directly ahead) keeping the remains of the ice works on the R.

1 Sourton Tors Ice Works

Before the days of mechanical refrigeration ice was in great demand for preserving food and particularly by fishmongers in Plymouth. The Sourton Tors Ice Works dates from about 1875 and lasted about ten years. The site lay 1300–1400 feet (396–426 m) above sea level and here water, a high incidence of frost, exposure to cold winds and easy access for horse and cart, all facilitated the development of this industry.

Water was channelled from a reliable hillside spring into as many as thirty shallow, rectangular pits or ponds in which ice would form during the winter months. The ice was cut into

Dartmoor's north western edge, on Arms Tor (left) and Brat Tor (right).

Widgery Cross on Brat Tor.

blocks and stored in a nearby granite building which would have been insulated with earth and turf. In a cool summer the ice supplies would last through to July. The time it took to transport the ice from the works to Plymouth must have meant that considerable wastage occurred.

2 *Branscombe's Loaf*

The thirteenth-century Bishop Walter Bronescombe made many excursions throughout his diocese which included far-flung places such as Lydford. This often meant traversing the open moors of Dartmoor. On one particular excursion he and his companions felt tired and hungry and on the wind-battered Corn Ridge he was approached by a cloaked stranger on horseback. The stranger offered the Bishop bread and cheese if he would get off his horse, take off his cap and call him 'Master'. The Bishop almost obliged but, in time it seems, an accompanying servant noticed the stranger's cloven hoof, whereupon the Bishop cried out to God and made the sign of the cross. The stranger instantly vanished leaving the bread and cheese turned to stone—the granite rock-piles of Branscombe's Loaf.

3 *Black-a-tor Copse*

Black-a-tor Copse (Beare) is the northernmost and highest of the three primeval woodlands on Dartmoor. The wood itself covers an area of 14 acres (5.7 ha) on the south-west-facing valley-side of the West Okement River, its altitude being between 1181 and 1443 feet (360–440 m). The trees of this pedunculate oakwood are distinctive in growth, form and height. Some are procumbent while upright trees are from 6½ to 40 feet (2–12 m) tall, most being gnarled and twisted.

4 *Rattlebrook peat workings*

The head basin of the Rattlebrook has been the scene of the largest commercial peat cutting on Dartmoor—and a century of activity saw the largest expenditure and subsequent loss of such ventures. The first extraction of peat here began in the 1850s. Packhorse transport and then horse-drawn carts conveyed the peat from the moors.

In 1878 the West of England Compressed Peat Company was granted a licence by the Duchy of Cornwall for peat extraction and the construction of a railway. In 1879 the Rattlebrook Peat Railway, of standard 4 feet 8½ in gauge, was completed. This 5¾-mile (9.2-km) long line joined the London and South West Railway near Bridestone and rising to 1800 feet (549 m) above sea level it can be truly described as a mountain railway. Horse drawn trucks conveyed both freight and workers to and from the works. The extracted products were used for gas, smelting and fertilizing. This venture lasted two years. Peat production continued until 1956. The long scars of peat cutting ties are clearly visible on the west-facing slope of Amicombe Hill.

5 *Great Links Tor*

Great Links Tor rises to 1923 feet (586 m) above sea level and resembles an ancient castle on the approach from the north-east. From its summit are views to two seas—the Bristol Channel and the English Channel—and to Cornwall's in-country rising to Bodmin Moor, and much of Dartmoor is taken in including the dome of Three Barrows in the Erme Valley on the southern moor.

6 *The River Tavy*

The River Tavy is famed for its wild beauty, its treeless cleave and for its swiftness—one of the most rapid in Britain. The river rises from blanket bog in the heart of Dartmoor at an altitude of 1840 feet (561 m) and falls a thousand feet (305 m) in seven miles (11 km); within the cleave the valley drops 300 feet (96 m) in 2 miles (3.2 km). The valley sides are clitter-strewn with five massive castellated tors on the north western slopes. The river has exploited the natural horizontal and vertical joints in the granite to cut the ravine and form numerous step-like waterfalls and pools including the 7-foot (2.1-m) fall into the 'Devil's Kitchen'.

7 *Doe Tor Brook tin streamings*

In the combe of Doe Tor Brook are extensive spoils from medieval tin streaming and the remains of the nineteenth-century Foxhole Tin Mine. Here is a leat, a fine masonry-built launder bank, a wheel-pit, buddle, tail-race and the mine house—the latter having two rooms each with a fireplace still surviving. The window openings and the front doorstep remain. This was principally a surface-working mine and water has been leated and diverted in many places to wash out gerts and expose the tin-bearing ore.

8 *Brat Tor Cross*

On the summit of Brat (pronounced 'Bray') Tor is the massive granite cross erected by painter William Widgery in honour of Queen Victoria's Golden Jubilee in 1887. This cross stands 13 feet (4 m) above the granite bedrock. William Widgery was born in South Molton, on Exmoor, in 1822. He worked as a stone mason and plasterer before becoming a full-time artist.

9 *Great Nodden*

Great Nodden rises to 1434 feet (437 m) above sea level. The entire ridge is of metamorphic slate and rises precipitously from the Dartmoor granite's western boundary on the valley floor of the River Lyd.

4.13

Shapley Common— Grimspound—Hamel Down—Corndon Tor —Birch Tor

STARTING AND FINISHING POINT

Shapley Common (191-698835). From Moretonhampstead follow B3212 towards Princetown for just over 4 miles. Pass over cattle grid and turn immediately R into large car-park on the next bend.

LENGTH

16¼ miles (26 km)

ASCENT

Four climbs: 1½ miles (2.4 km), ascent 433 ft (132 m) to Hookney Tor; ⅓ mile (0.5 km), ascent 260 ft (79 m) to Hameldown Tor; 1¼ miles (2.0 km), ascent 636 ft (194 m) to Corndon Tor; 1 mile (1.5 km), ascent 357 ft (109 m) to Birch Tor.

This circular route allows a walk along all of the continuous, north to south running ridge comprising Shapley Common, Hamel Down, Dunstone Down and Bittleford Down—a distance of 5½ miles (8.8 km).

The walk includes four steep climbs and traverses open moorland. It follows, in part, a riverside footpath and a right of way through a conifer plantation. It also includes some 1½ miles (2.5 km) lane and road walking.

ROUTE DESCRIPTION (Maps 19—22)

From the car-park cross over the road to follow the path rising up over Shapley Common, keeping the stone wall boundaries well to the L. On these lower slopes the route passes three massive prehistoric hut circles. Follow a prehistoric boundary work (a reave) up the slope until it peters out and head for the summit pile of Shapley Tor. Follow a clear path to Hookney Tor *(1)* crossing straight over a fallen, redundant stone wall.

A severely eroded path drops down to the huge circular prehistoric settlement of Grimspound situated on the southern slopes of the Grims Lake Valley *(2)*. The combination of horses' hoofs, walkers' boots and rain run-off has created a linear scar running down from the tor so, to help avoid further wear, pick your own route down through the heather to the settlement. Pass through the 'village' of Grimspound and leave the main gateway in the south-east wall for a short but steep climb straight ahead to Hameldown Tor.

The walk continues southwards along the ridge of Hamel Down to Wind Tor, a distance of 3 miles (5 km) and offers views of south-east and west Dartmoor and of south Devon.

Keep the OS Triangulation Point on the tor to the R and go straight on following a wide track which passes the remains of Hamel Down Cross (on R) *(3)* and the summit, prehistoric burial cairns of Broad Barrow, Single Barrow and—keeping Blackaton Down improved enclosure on the R—Two Barrows and Hameldown Beacon *(4)*.

From Hameldown Beacon the path descends to the enclosures of Kingshead and Coombe lying above Widecombe-in-the-Moor *(5)*; keep the wall on the L and continue straight on (fingerpost, 'To Widecombe'). Where the wall eventually bends around and drops down to the L the path divides; go straight on ignoring track waymarked 'To Widecombe'. Cross the lane, which drops down to Widecombe-in-the-Moor, and go straight on over Dunstone Down. Where the track divides bear half R for the small outcrop of Wind Tor. Continue straight on (south) over Bittleford Down and turn half R on approaching field boundaries. Cross over the lane and cut straight over a further area of common until reaching the Jordan and Shallowford Lane. Go R onto the lane and follow to the crossroads where there is a small medieval cross (R); turn L and continue along the lane, passing Drywell (on R), to the hamlet of Jordan.

Prehistoric hut circle, Shapley Common.

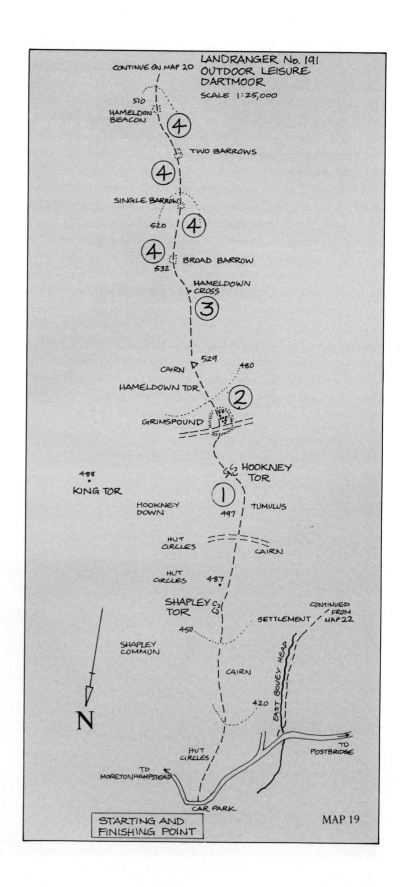

LANDRANGER No. 191
OUTDOOR LEISURE
DARTMOOR
SCALE 1:25,000

CONTINUE ON MAP 20

510

HAMELDON
BEACON

④

TWO BARROWS

④

SINGLE BARROW

520

④

④
532

BROAD BARROW

HAMELDOWN
CROSS

③

529

CAIRN   480

HAMELDOWN TOR

②

GRIMSPOUND

488
•
KING TOR

HOOKNEY
TOR

HOOKNEY
DOWN

①

TUMULUS

497

HUT
CIRCLES

CAIRN

HUT
CIRCLES   487

SHAPLEY
TOR

CONTINUED
FROM
MAP 22

SETTLEMENT

450

SHAPLEY
COMMON

CAIRN

420

EAST BOVEY HEAD

N

TO
POSTBRIDGE

HUT
CIRCLES

TO
MORETONHAMPSTEAD

CAR PARK

STARTING AND
FINISHING POINT

MAP 19

104

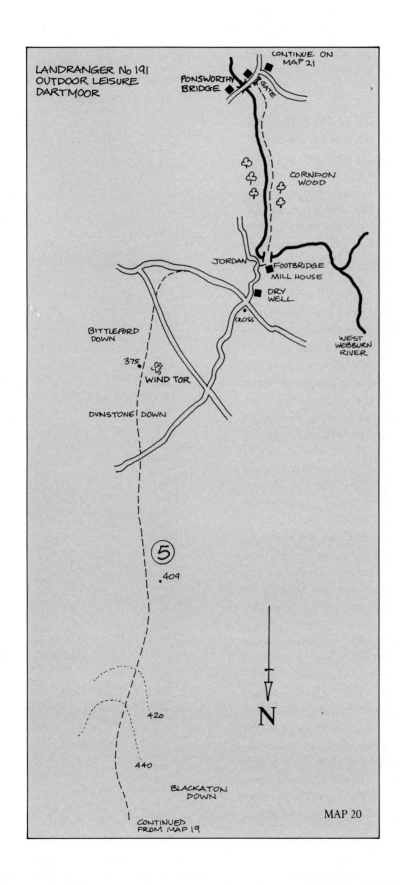

LANDRANGER No 191
OUTDOOR LEISURE
DARTMOOR

CONTINUE ON
MAP 21

PONSWORTHY
BRIDGE

GATE

CORNDON
WOOD

JORDAN

FOOTBRIDGE
MILL HOUSE

DRY
WELL

CROSS

BITTLEFORD
DOWN

WEST
WEBBURN
RIVER

375.

WIND TOR

DUNSTONE DOWN

⑤

.409

N

420

440

BLACKATON
DOWN

MAP 20

CONTINUED
FROM MAP 19

At Jordan, ignore a turning on the L, and carry on for a short distance along the lane signposted 'No through road'. At Mill House and Jordan Cottage go left (PFS 'County Road at Ponsworthy ¼ ml'). The footpath goes between the two cottages and over a footbridge which spans the West Webburn River. After the bridge take an obvious path keeping the river to the L. Follow the riverside path, ignoring a wide forestry track on the R which climbs above Corndon Wood. On reaching the end of the footpath at Ponsworthy, go through the gate by the cottage. If you want the village post office and stores (a sign describes it as 'a brandy to boot laces village shop') turn L, cross the ford, and go L again; the shop is on the R just above the road bridge which crosses the river. Otherwise, at the lane go R and walk up the lane to Lock's Gate Cross.

At the crossroads go straight on (highway sign 'Dartmeet and Princetown') taking the path running parallel to the lane on the R side verge. Where the field boundaries end abruptly to the R, follow the path round and ascend Corndon Tor (half L).

From the summit of Corndon Tor are fine views including one of the ancient tenement of Babeny. Pass a prehistoric stone cairn and continue straight on along the crest of the ridge heading for two more massive stone cairns. Go roughly straight on but slightly to the left, crossing several prehistoric reaves and head in line with the distant Fernworthy Forest which edges its way over the furthest horizon. Bear half L when Riddon and Wild Goose settlements come into full view and walk down-slope to reach a well-defined track; turn R and follow to the lane. Go L onto the lane and follow. Continue straight on at Cator Green T junction (highway signed 'Bellever'). After about a further ¼ mile (0.4 km) of lane walking, at the far end of a large beech shelter-belt, go through a gate immediately on the R and keep on the bridlepath across Cator Common heading for Soussons plantation; a PBS confirms the route halfway over this open area.

On reaching an ancient track which leads to Pizwell (on the L) *(6)* go through the gate and cut straight over to the road heading for a large ride within the conifer plantation. On the other side of the road is a small area which escaped coniferization and here is a fine prehistoric cairn circle tucked closely to the plantation perimeter. Retrace your steps to the lane. Go left along the lane past Ephraim's Pinch *(7)* and at the granite gate posts, around the next bend, go half L on a path through a beech, oak and pine wood. This leads onto open ground to pick up a track to Soussons Farm, a Forestry Commission holding on a lease from the Duchy of Cornwall which is tenanted out.

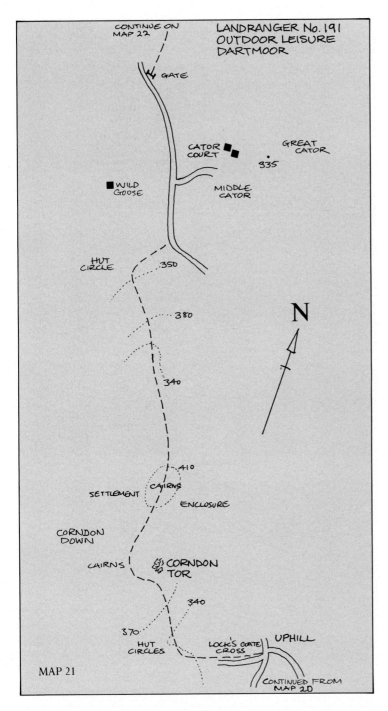

CONTINUE ON MAP 22

LANDRANGER No. 191
OUTDOOR LEISURE
DARTMOOR

GATE

CATOR COURT

GREAT CATOR

335

WILD GOOSE

MIDDLE CATOR

HUT CIRCLE

350

380

N

340

410

CAIRNS

SETTLEMENT

ENCLOSURE

CORNDON DOWN

CAIRNS

CORNDON TOR

340

370

HUT CIRCLES

LOCK'S GATE CROSS

UPHILL

MAP 21

CONTINUED FROM MAP 20

At the farm do not turn R through the farmyard, but go through the gate and turn R (PFS 'Challacombe'). Follow the edge of the field round and follow the fence line up the hill. At the top of the field go through a gate and turn R onto a track running parallel with a stone wall (on R). Cross the stone bridge over the stream and follow the path straight on. At the next gate

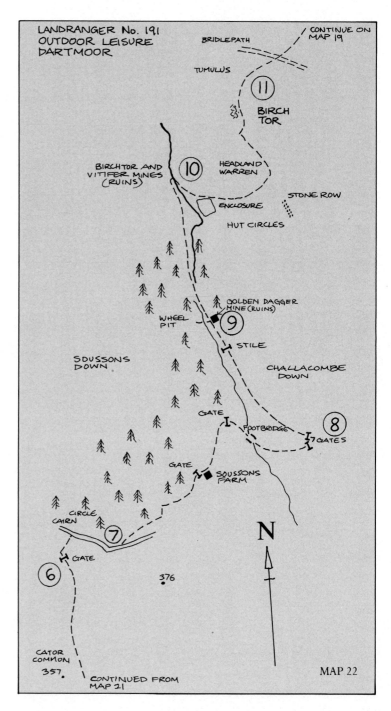

continue in the same direction (towards Hamel Down ridge) and when Challacombe Farm, a Duchy holding, comes into view go through a gate and turn immediately L to go through another gate to follow a footpath (PFS 'Bennett's B3212 Cross'—as spelt on the OS map) *(8)*. Keeping on this path continue around the lower slopes of the bracken-infested western flank of

Challacombe Down. On reaching the forest edge, go over a stile (PFS) passing the remains of Golden Dagger (tin) Mine *(9)*. After a ruined building on the L, a small overgrown path drops down and crosses the infant river, via a small granite bridge, and leads up to the walled structure of a disused wheel pit—well worth a visit, but take care as it is quite deep. Retrace your steps to the footpath, turn L and head upstream along the valley bottom. Where the path emerges from the forest go straight on and pass the stream-side willows; ignore paths to the L and R. A path-bridlepath junction is soon encountered; continue in the same direction (PBS 'Bennett's Cross B3212') on what can be a muddy stretch. The small fenced-in areas, by the bridlepath, here warn us of disused mining shafts—keep well away. Go through the gate, continue straight on along the bridlepath for about 550 yards (503 m) to reach a relatively broad level area in the valley bottom. Here are the remains of the Birch Tor/Vitifer Tin Mines complex *(10)*. On reaching this level ground a line of telegraph poles cuts the valley bottom. On encountering the first pole on the R, walk 75 yards (64 m) and then follow the track (a bridlepath) leading off on the R uphill. This track runs roughly parallel with the lines of telegraph poles on the L and the wall of an abandoned enclosure on the R for a short distance.

Where the bridlepath levels out continue in the same direction until the prehistoric triple stone row on Challacombe Down ridge is immediately on the R. Here, turn L to leave the bridlepath and follow a small path weaving its way through bracken and heather and bilberry to Birch Tor *(11)*. From this granite pile much of the walk so far accomplished comes into view. Continue straight on along the path over the summit passing a cairn and a small granite warren bondstone on the L. At the west–east running bridlepath go R and follow until reaching another warren bondstone on the R, next to some tinners' trial pits and gullies. Leave the bridlepath here, turning half L (the orientation of a trial gully working here gives the direction needed; there is no path to follow across the down). With the Widecombe-in-the-Moor to Challacombe Lane in view go to East Bovey Head to encounter the source of the river. A walk in summer here to reach the combe floor will mean some bracken-wading. Keep the infant river to the R and follow the left bank downstream. On reaching the Moretonhampstead to Postbridge road cross over the river by the road bridge to avoid boggy ground. Continue along the left verge of the main road to return to the car-park.

1 Hookney Tor

The 360-degrees view from the Hookney Tor is magnificent. A 20-mile (32-km) north to south span of Dartmoor includes

Brent Hill, Ryder's Hill, Caters Beam and Eylesbarrow on the southern moors and the lofty skyline of Cut Hill, Whitehorse Hill, Hangingstone Hill, High Willhays, Yes Tor, and the smooth-domed skyline of Cosdon Hill, to the north west. Due north the Exmoor range can be seen on the distant horizon. Shallow leats have been cut by tinners on the tor's southern flank to collect hillside drainage and stream flow from Grims Lake; this water was conducted to the huge gerts of Headland Mine for washing out lodes.

2 *Grimspound*

Grimspound is probably the best known collection of prehistoric hut circles—24 in all—on Dartmoor and lies 1530 feet (470 m) above sea level. Some believed this four-acre (1.6 ha) site to be a temple of the sun, others a fortified settlement. Despite its massive enclosing wall, clearly the village's position on the slopes of a hill flanked by tors was not defensive.

The surviving remains of this village have been altered by subsequent peoples. For example, the vast perimeter wall, now about nine feet (2.5 m) in width, has been restored as regards its height in the recent past and what appears to be an entrance on the lower, west side, is the result of generations of tinners and moormen and, for the last hundred years, visitors, passing through.

3 *Hamel Down Cross*

The rudely-fashioned Hamel Down Cross bears on its east face:

HC

DS

1854

This inscription refers to the name of the cross and the Duke of Somerset. At that time the Duke owned Natsworthy Manor in the East Webburn valley and it was he who had the ancient cross adapted as a manor boundstone. Further on along the ridge more 'DS stones' were set up including one on each of the four barrows to the south of the cross.

4 *Hamel Down and the Beacon*

Around 2000 BC stone rows and small cairns appear to have been succeeded by the large cairns and barrows which can be striking features of the Dartmoor skyline. These were burial mounds of the more important families, some of whom were buried with copper or bronze weapons. On Hamel Down, at about 1735 feet (529 m) above sea level, is a cemetery consisting of four sizeable barrows.

In a mid-sixteenth-century document specifying the

Opposite: *A small wood near Ephraim's Pinch.*

Following page: *Headland Warren and Birch Tor.*

Natsworthy Manor bounds, Hameldon Beacon appears as 'Fyerbicken'. Tradition records that this signal hill was fired when the Armada was sighted in the English Channel.

5 *Widecombe-in-the-Moor*

Widecombe-in-the-Moor lies within the sweeping vale of the East Webburn River. To the west of the village the ridge of Hamel Down separates this valley from that of the West Webburn. St. Pancras Church, known as 'the cathedral of the moor', was built in the fourteenth century on the site of an earlier church and then was enlarged and the 120-foot (36.6-m) tower added in the fifteenth or early sixteenth century. The magnificence of the tower is attributed to the financial support of tin miners who exploited all the surrounding valleys for the rich ore.

6 *Pizwell*

Pizwell was first documented as a tenement cluster of three farms in 1260. Previous to this date it is known that families living here had to use the parish church at Lydford on west Dartmoor until dispensation was granted, by Bishop Bronescombe, to use the church at Widecombe-in-the-Moor—a distance of 3½ miles (5.6 km), being considerably shorter than the distance to Lydford. The route to Widecombe became established as one of the many church paths on Dartmoor.

7 *Ephraim's Pinch*

Ephraim's Pinch is reputed to be so-called after a man named Ephraim who laid a wager that he could carry a sack of corn from Widecombe-in-the-Moor to Postbridge, a distance of 5 miles (8 km), without dropping it. After 3½ miles (5.6 km) he reached this spot and he found the *pinch* too much for him and threw his burden on the ground thus losing his bet.

8 *Challacombe Farm*

A shrinkage of the medieval hamlet here has occurred either because of the Black Death or because of climatic deterioration. The hamlet once had at least seven dwellings but is now occupied by a farmhouse and two cottages.

The slopes of Challacombe Down are infested with bracken. Bracken is believed to have spread in recent years on a wide scale not just on Dartmoor but throughout the world. It is known to be carcinogenic to cattle, and possibly to man, and is ecologically poorer than the moorland plant communities it takes over; it also looks at its best when dead. The Duchy of Cornwall, with the co-operation of its tenant farmer at Challacombe and the National Park Authority are undertaking an extensive and detailed series of bracken control experiments.

9 Golden Dagger Mine

The last tin mine to work on Dartmoor was at Golden Dagger. Underground work had stopped at the time of the First World War, but exploitation of the waste heaps left by earlier generations of tinners continued until 12 November 1930 when the firm operating at that time closed the mine.

The mine almost certainly had a medieval origin but the first record of the name 'Golden Dagger' dates from 1851.

Along the path through the plantation there are remains of old buildings, a wheelpit, leat systems and three circular buddles where crushed tin ore was concentrated. On the opposite side of the (Redwater Brook) valley another wheelpit can be seen; this, together with the remains of the Mine Captain's House, was consolidated by the National Park Authority in March 1982 to prevent further deterioration. Not all the shafts have been filled in so do not venture off the paths.

10 Birch Tor tin workings

Some of the most extensive tin working activity on Dartmoor took place in the Birch Tor area. Here are the waste heaps of alluvial workings, or streamworks, in the valleys and the vast man-made gullies where lode ore was exploited by open cast workings and later by shaft mining. Two separate mines, Birch Tor and Vitifer existed here but for most of their working lives from 1858 they operated as one. Some of the open cast workings are probably medieval in origin and deep shafts were sunk in the bottom in the eighteenth and nineteenth centuries. The first record of a mine here dates to 1750. The foundations of the mine carpenter's shop, blacksmith's shop, the 'Miner's House'—where workers could stay for a week in dormitories—the Mine Captain's House and several cottages still survive. The remains of wheelpits and dressing floors containing the foundations of buddles can also be seen.

11 Birch Tor

Birch Tor itself stands 1598 feet (487 m) above sea level. Below the tor are four enclosures known as 'Jan Reynolds' Cards' or the 'Aces'. In the southernmost, the miners grew vegetables and in others the warreners of Headland Warren grew furze as food for rabbits. Legend has it that Jan Reynolds was carried off by the Devil for playing cards in Widecombe Church and dropped the four aces as he was taken over Birch Tor. From the tor several warren boundstones bearing the letters 'WB' will be encountered.

4.14

THE NORTHERN WILDERNESS

STARTING AND FINISHING POINT

Large car-park at Postbridge (191-646788) on B3212, 3½ miles (5.5 km) north east of Two Bridges, 8½ miles (13.5 km) south west of Moretonhampstead. A Dartmoor National Park Information Centre (minimum opening period Easter–end of October–open daily) is situated here. Toilets and information board.

LENGTH

15½ miles (25 km)

ASCENT

Five climbs: 0.6 mile (1 km), ascent 215 ft (65 m) to East Dart Waterfall; ⅓ mile (0.5 km), ascent 128 ft (39 m) to Statts House; ⅓ mile (0.5 km), ascent 164 ft (50 m) to Quintin's Man; 1 mile (1.5 km), ascent 170 ft (52 m) to summit of Whitehorse Hill; ⅓ mile (0.5 km), ascent 360 ft (110 m) to Fur Tor.

This walk crosses a wilderness equal to that of any other British moorland—Dartmoor's great northern fen. The route follows the East Dart River upstream to Sandy Hole Pass and over Winney's Down and Whitehorse Hill to Hangingstone Hill and thence to Cranmere Pool. The return is via Fur Tor and Cut Hill. The walk, in part, lies within the Okehampton and Merrivale Firing Ranges; check the firing programme before setting out. Do not attempt the walk in misty weather. The demanding terrain, the distance covered and the vegetation combine to make this a very strenuous walk.

ROUTE DESCRIPTION (Maps 23—25)

From the car-park turn L onto the main Moretonhampstead to Two Bridges road and pass the Post Office and Village Stores (on L); go over the road bridge which runs parallel to the medieval clapper bridge *(1)*. Turn immediately L after the bridge through a hunting gate, immediately next to a five-bar gate. Pass through this field following the wall (R) towards Ringhill, then turn L and follow the wall to the river, passing Hartyland (R). Go through a hunting gate here and turn R to continue on upstream, passing through another two gates in the small plantation near Hartyland.

On entering Hartland Tor Newtake the path runs straight up the East Dart Valley close to the river bank passing below Hartland Tor. Cross the stile over the stone wall at the far side of the newtake to enter the extensive Stannon Tor Newtake. Continue on near the river until a tributary stream (Lade Hill Bottom) flows in from the north (R) near to where the East Dart River swings abruptly to the L. On the opposite side of the river can be seen a take-off point for a leat which ran to Powder Mills; the dry leat contours its way down the valley. Cross over the stream near to where it enters the East Dart River above a weir. Continue on in the same direction following a path uphill

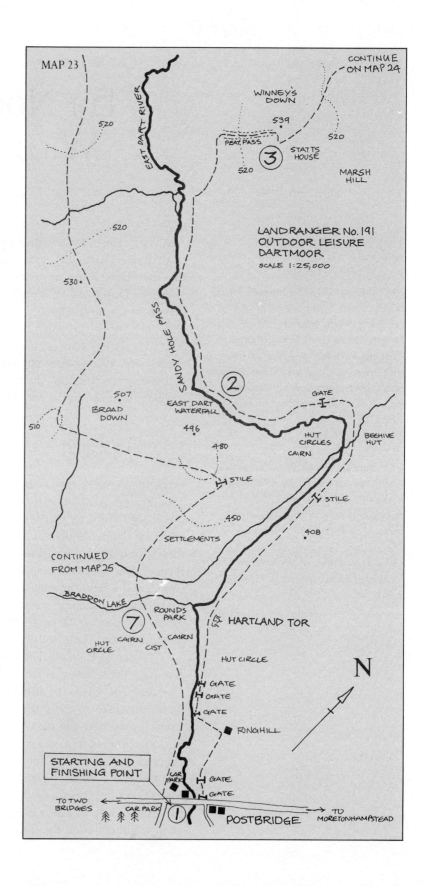

MAP 23

CONTINUE
ON MAP 24

EAST DART RIVER

520

WINNEY'S
DOWN

539

520

PEAT PASS

3

STATTS
HOUSE

520

MARSH
HILL

LANDRANGER No. 191
OUTDOOR LEISURE
DARTMOOR

SCALE 1:25,000

520

530·

SANDY HOLE PASS

507·
BROAD
DOWN

510

530·

2

EAST DART
WATERFALL

GATE

HUT
CIRCLES

BEEHIVE
HUT

496·

CAIRN

480

STILE

STILE

450

408·

SETTLEMENTS

CONTINUED
FROM MAP 25

BRADDON LAKE

7

ROUNDS
PARK

HARTLAND TOR

HUT
CIRCLE

CAIRN

CAIRN

CIST

HUT CIRCLE

N

GATE

GATE

GATE

RINGHILL

STARTING AND
FINISHING POINT

CAR
PARK

GATE

GATE

TO TWO
BRIDGES

CAR PARK

1

POSTBRIDGE

TO
MORETONHAMPSTEAD

which, in its turn, soon veers to the L, and follow the East Dart upstream. Go through the gate and, staying on the path, cross Winney's Down Brook. Follow a path round the L side of the hill to reach the base of the East Dart Waterfall *(2)*.

Staying on the river's L bank continue up the valley to the narrow defile of Sandy Hole Pass, passing extensive tin-streaming spoils on the L. Keep on the path running over the top of Sandy Hole Pass. Here the valley opens out into Broad Marsh. Continue straight on the path which runs above the flood plain and follow this path which eventually skirts round half R to avoid boggy ground. The path soon becomes poorly-defined through the luxuriant grass growth; head straight on in the direction of a shallow coombe and on approach turn R uphill to follow the peat pass to Statts House *(3)*, a ruined peat cutter's house, on Winney's Down.

Continue along the crest of the Down (northwards) in the direction of Quintin's Man—which comprises stable and look-out hut and summit cairn—passing the remains of another peat cutter's home on the L. Drop down into the infant valley of the South Teign River and, keeping the Range poles and Notice Board on the L, cross the river and continue on upslope following the Range poles. From the look-out hut on Quintin's Man continue straight on along a military track which runs north-north eastwards and keep the Range poles here well to the R. On Whitehorse Hill summit the military track is granite-paved and it swings away to the R through a peat pass; keep on this track for about 260 yards (237 m) and then cut L to contour around to the lowly tor on Hangingstone Hill. The flat area between Whitehorse and Hangingstone Hills is extremely boggy and should be avoided. From the observation post turn L onto a small path leading towards Taw Head. Cross above the bluff at the very head of the River Taw and continue almost half R over the highest rise of the hill here. The level boggy area to the L of Taw Head, the birth-place of the East Dart River, must be avoided. From the top of the hill it is possible to discern the shallow depression, roughly oval in shape, of Cranmere Pool. Beyond the pool lies the easternmost branch of West Okement Head and further still Great Links Tor.

Make your way to Cranmere Pool, the 'post-box' being surrounded by granite paving slabs *(4)*. This is a wild place; the fens have given rise to many of Devon's rivers. Features are few and many people search for the letterbox without any success. Good visibility is essential. After signing the visitors' book, carry straight on over the hill ahead, keeping West Okement Head to the R. Halfway up the hill can be seen a large cutting in the peat to the L—the Black Ridge Peat Pass *(5)*. Cut across to the peat pass marker post and follow on up on to Black Ridge whereupon the 'cut' opens out; small stone cairns confirm the route through the peat hags where the crossing is open. Follow the pass which is some 1100 yards (1006 m) long, heading for Fur Tor.

At the end of the pass continue in the direction of Fur Tor, which lies directly ahead, and drop down to Black Ridge Brook. Cross over the stream and turn R to walk downstream for about 200 yards (183 m) until picking a dry route on the L to avoid marshy ground. When above the marsh bear left again and

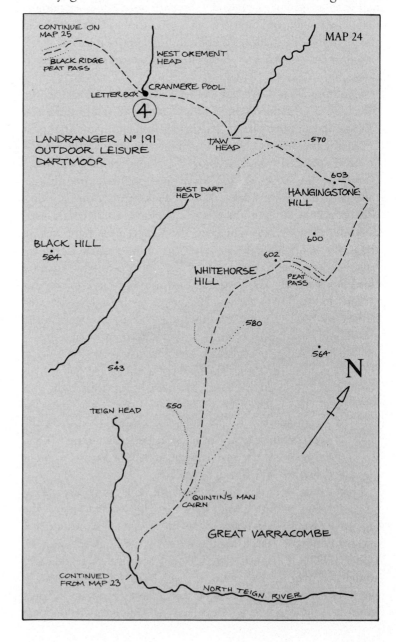

follow the side of the hill for a further 300 yards (274 m) to pick up another peat pass on the R which cuts across the eastern side (lowest end) of Little Kneeset. This pass is less obvious than that of Black Ridge but, rising over the crest of the hill, Fur Tor reappears in view. Aiming for the L side of Fur Tor drop down to Cut Combe Water. Cross the stream and make for the summit of Fur Tor *(6)* by first heading for the left pile. Then ascend by traversing the hillside to half R. From the western pile go past the main rock pile and continue straight on keeping the head of the southern bank of Cut Combe Water on the L. Follow the

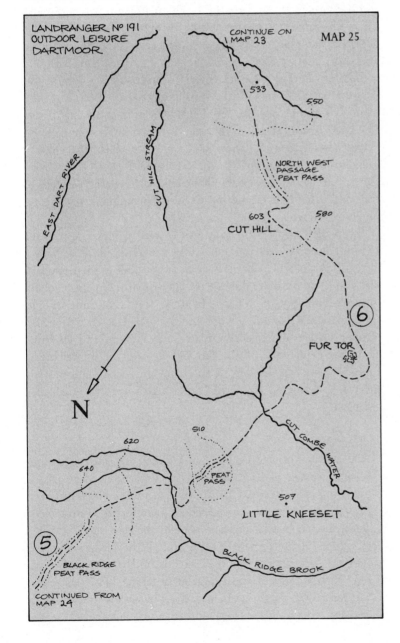

path, flanked by Range poles, leading up to Cut Hill.

On Cut Hill, turn R at Range Notice Boards and walk due south, in the direction of the radio mast on North Hessary Tor, for about 150 yards (137 m). On reaching the North West Passage peat pass, the beginning of which is marked by two small stone cairns, turn L and follow the pass—also with marker cairns—downslope. At the end of the pass continue on downslope along a little-used path keeping the source of the West Dart River over to the R. Aim for the left of two Range poles ahead on a spur and keep the valleys of Cut Hill Stream and the East Dart River on the L. The path soon peters out and the walk here is quite demanding through grass tussocks and humps. Cross the stream and go in the same direction over the next hill crest passing the Range pole. Cross a sizeable gully containing tinners' spoil heaps and go on towards a combe, the head of which is on the R. A pronounced path runs from the combe over the opposite hill—head for this and follow over. The path disappears, but continue in the same direction. With Fernworthy Forest and the East Dart Waterfall in the view to the L, continue on along the same contour to head over Broad Down. On having passed the defile below the waterfall begin to rise over the Down and head for a prominent prehistoric vegetated cairn.

From the cairn, cut down to half L, over a combe, aiming for a granite outcrop near to the newtake wall. Follow the wall until it bends to the R. Cross the stile here and follow the boundary wall (on L) downslope; this is a permitted path. On approaching Breddon Lake Bottom the wall bends to the L; continue straight on crossing old boundary work and over the leat via a nine slab clapper bridge. Go over Breddon Lake Bottom and continue along the bridlepath. With Hartland Tor on the immediate L, Roundy Park kistvaen lies in an enclosure. Continue on along the track, known as the Drift Lane (7) to return to Postbridge car-park.

1 Postbridge

The village of Postbridge dates from the late eighteenth century when in 1772 two Acts of Parliament were passed allowing the formation of the Moretonhampstead and Tavistock Turnpike Trusts. These two Trusts contracted a local moorman and his sons to build the new road, which is the basis of the present B3212, and all the bridges along its length. A toll house was built at Postbridge to recover costs and in the 1820s it was reported as taking £100 per year.

Before the road was built a trans-moorland track already existed and at Postbridge a ford and a medieval clapper

Opposite: Postbridge clapper bridge, spanning the East Dart river.

bridge crossed the East Dart River. Postbridge Clapper Bridge is built of massive slabs of granite and one of the earliest written records to it is in 1675, although it was built some 400 years earlier.

2 *East Dart Waterfall*

Between the upper and middle reaches of the East Dart River is one of the most outstanding waterfalls on Dartmoor. The fall occurs diagonally across the river bed which the river has deeply incised.

3 *Winney's Down*

On the summit of Winney's Down (really known as Marsh Hill) at some 1768 feet (529 m) above sea level is the ruin of Statt's House. It comprises a curved north wall and a squared wall with a fireplace and alcove at the south. It was probably built in the eighteenth century by Stat(t) the turf-cutter as a shelter.

4 *Cranmere Pool*

Famed in legend, and in past and present Dartmoor guide books, Cranmere Pool was once a water-filled peat bog, but it was breached sometime in the early nineteenth century either by storm water or by, some say, a shepherd who found the small tarn dangerous for sheep. A seventeenth-century Mayor of Okehampton, a Benjamin ('Binjy') Gayer (Gear) was convicted of sheep stealing and was said to be hanged at Hangingstone Hill. His spirit was banished to Cranmere Pool there to empty it with a sieve until the task was accomplished, which he evidently did.

From the outset of the Romantic movement, art and literature had been instrumental in creating an appreciation of 'wildness', and with improving communications, Britain's uplands, including Dartmoor, started to become tourist attractions. The first known guided 'visitor' to Cranmere Pool was a certain John Andrews who made his journey on 11 August 1789. Sixty-five years later, in 1854, James Perrott of Chagford set up a small cairn on the now relatively dry bed of the pool; in it he put a glass jar where visitors who had ventured to this lonely and bleak spot could leave their visiting cards. By 1889 a tin box replaced the jar. In April 1905, two moorland ramblers placed a visitors' book in the box. In the first nine months this received 609 signatures and, by 1908, 1741 signatures were recorded.

The pilgrimage grew and in 1912 the first 'letterbox', which was made in Chagford, was built into the bank of the pool after being sledded (sledged) to the site. In 1937 the Western Morning News launched an appeal for funds to inaugurate a more permanent postal arrangement. Aubrey

A granite outcrop on Winney's Down.

Tucker, a carpenter and ex-Dartmoor tin miner from Sticklepath, was commissioned to construct a permanent letterbox. This was built of granite blocks taken from Belstone Tors. It still stands today.

Thus grew the phenomenon of letterboxing on Dartmoor; and such was its popularity that in 1987 the Dartmoor National Park Authority had to place granite slabs around the Cranmere Pool box to remedy, and prevent further, erosion. The number of letterboxes on Dartmoor has risen to upward of 1500, although not all are permanent.

5 *The Peat Passes of Marsh Hill and Black Ridge*

Northern Dartmoor contains vast areas of blanket bog and artificial peat passes have been cut to link one dry hillside with another. Each pass has its own name and the oldest is Cut Lane which connects the West Dart Valley with that of the Tavy and may have been cut in Saxon times.

Marsh Hill Peat Pass is some 350 yards (320 m) long and contains one or two sections of causeway. Whitehorse Hill pass is 270 yards (247 m) long and was widened and cleared

in 1963 by a bulldozer when a military track was being made. On Black Ridge the peat pass is some 1100 yards (1006 m) in length and is the longest. The sides of the passes are constantly eroded by weather and animals and, where causeways have been laid, gutters have to be cleared. Such maintenance work has been carried out by volunteers organized by the Mid-Devon Hunt.

6 *Fur Tor*

Within the fastness of north Dartmoor's blanket bog there is but one tor—Fur Tor. The tor rises dramatically to 1877 feet (572 m) above sea level. It is spoken of as 'Vurtor'—the 'great tor', the 'far distant tor'.

7 *Drift Lane*

Running down from Chittaford Down and Broadun to Postbridge is a wide lane which is known as the Drift Lane and is part of an ancient north–south trans-Dartmoor track.

Beech shelterbelt near Archerton.

1.15

A CIRCUIT OF DUNSTER PARK

STARTING AND FINISHING
POINT
Car-park on south side of Dunster
Castle near Gallox Bridge (181-
990433).
LENGTH
3 miles (4.8 km)
ASCENT
700 ft (213 m)

A pleasant walk on the edge of Exmoor's most attractive small town through woods and a one-time deer park belonging to Dunster Castle. Deer may still be seen, but they are no longer confined to the park. There are fine views of the Castle, and the walk passes through two prehistoric earthworks.

ROUTE DESCRIPTION (Map 26)

Leave the car-park on the south side of Dunster Castle, and take the short footpath going downhill to the ancient crossing of the small river Avill known as Gallox Bridge *(1)*. Cross the bridge and walk past a thatched cottage to Park Gate, a junction of several tracks.

Take the track signposted 'Timberscombe 3, Luxborough 5 via Croydon Hill'. This is a broad, gently-rising track through mixed woodland and is waymarked yellow and blue. Where the track levels out, ignore a gated path L. The route to follow is straight ahead and is waymarked. Take the L track at a fork. This rises further and bears L and is the Old Coach Road *(2)*. At a sharp bend to the L, leave the track for a viewpoint a short distance to the R *(3)*.

Return to the track and continue along it. About 150 yds (137 m) further on, turn acutely L up a climbing path, and 5 yds (4.5 m) before reaching a gate and stile pass through a hedge gap R and climb steeply up a path through young trees. The path reaches open moorland where there is much bracken. To the R of the path are the earthworks of a prehistoric enclosure *(4)*.

Carry on along this airy ridge path, descend to a saddle and climb beyond to Bat's Castle *(5)*. Pass through this earthwork and go down the other side on a broad grassy track towards a larch plantation. About 150 yds (137 m) into the plantation, at its far end, there is a path junction. Pass through a gate called Withycombe Hill Gate and turn L, ignoring a signpost before the gate reading 'Dunster'.

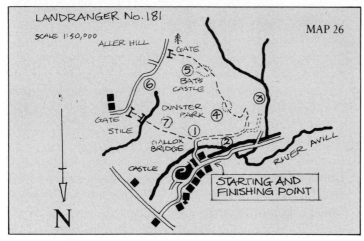

Bridge over the River Avill, looking towards Dunster deer park.

Follow this rough track downhill. The beech hedge on your L is known as the King's Hedge *(6)*. After nearly 1 mile (1.6 km) of walking down this track with the ancient wall on your L, where the track bends sharply R, turn L through a gate at a signpost reading 'Public Path Dunster'.

Dunster Castle stables.

The way is obvious across several fields through rolling parkland. This is the most recognizable section of the old deer park *(7)*. The outward leg of the route is eventually met, where you should turn R past the thatched cottages for Gallox Bridge and the start of the walk.

1 *Gallox Bridge*

A two-arched packhorse bridge once called Doddebridge. Carts used the ford. 'Gallox' means gallows, and there may have been a gallows nearby, or it could have been sited on the top of Gallox Hill, or both! Look for the smart little dipper flitting from stone to stone in the river.

2 *The Old Coach Road*

This was begun as a gently-graded carriage-way by Mr George Luttrell in the last century, and was meant to run from Dunster Castle to the Luxborough road, but funds ran out, and construction stopped at the viewpoint.

3 *The viewpoint*

The viewpoint at Black Ball is a delightful area of heather and scattered Scots' pine. Views extend up the Avill valley to Wootton Courtenay and Dunkery Beacon.

4 *Gallox Hill earthwork*

A small enclosure of less than 1 acre probably dating to Iron Age times, say 2,000 years ago. This is a good place for whortleberries in early September.

5 *Bat's Castle*

The origin of the name is not known, but its age is probably similar to its neighbour on Gallox Hill. It may have been refortified in the Civil War.

6 *King's Hedge*

The origin of the name is not known. Some authorities say it marked the boundary between the Royalists and the Parliamentarians in the Civil War. There are place names on Dartmoor known as the King Way, the King Wall and King's Gutter.

7 *Dunster Deer Park*

In medieval times deer were kept to the north-east of Dunster, but in 1755 Henry Fownes Luttrell emparked 348 acres to the south of the Castle. The purpose was what we would now term 'amenity', and the animals were culled and eaten. There are some fine old oaks still to be seen, and the views of Dunster Castle from this angle show it to its best advantage.

Doone Country and Brendon Common

STARTING AND FINISHING POINT
Exmoor National Park car-park at Malmsmead (180-793477).
LENGTH
5 miles (8 km)
ASCENT
600 ft (182 m)

A gentle walk with no tough climbs through moorland steeped in the Doone story. After following the Badgworthy (pronounced 'Badgery') Water upstream, the route veers away westwards to high open moorland where the indistinct track may be easily followed in clear weather but can be hard to trace when an Exmoor mist obscures everything except the immediate surroundings. Walkers are therefore advised to take a compass and be confident in its use. There are extensive views from the highest points, so it is best to reserve this walk for a day of good visibility.

Route Description (Map 27)

Leave the car-park at Malmsmead *(1)*, and take the uphill lane heading south signposted 'Fullinscott, Slocombeslade, Tippacott'. Where the lane bears R, enter the gate L, and follow the track signposted 'Public bridlepath to Doone Valley'. The route passes some mature ash trees L and jinks L and R but continues generally south along a well-defined waymarked track. It dips to Badgworthy Water where Cloud Farm is just across the river *(2)*.

Once past Cloud Farm the landscape becomes more open, the track is nearer the river, and there is more rock in evidence. A short distance further on a memorial stone to R. D. Blackmore is passed *(3)*, and then the track enters Yealscombe and Badgworthy Woods where oak and ash thrive.

The stream flowing down Lank Combe *(4)* is crossed by a footbridge in an attractive rocky glen in open woodland, and the path continues along a steep hillside, crossing Withycombe Ridge Water where a wonderful panorama opens out to the south. Across the river here is a stretch of moorland known as Deer Park *(5)*. The path soon reaches the foot of Hoccombe Combe where a prominent beech hedge crosses the foreground view, and where there is some tumbled ground.

Looking down to Malmsmead from near County Gate.

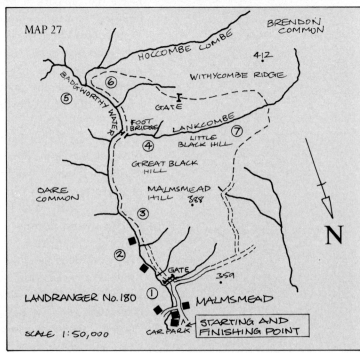

Turn away from Badgworthy Water here and pick up a well-used track heading in a general north-west direction. It at once passes a medieval village site *(6)* and climbs past a ruined cottage, and then the track dips to cross Withycombe Ridge Water and climbs to a gate in a wall. The track is now less distinct as it crosses the featureless plateau of Withycombe Ridge, part of Brendon Common. This is elemental Exmoor, an apparently flat tableland, but broken by countless small valleys. The headwaters of the stream flowing down Lank Combe are crossed at Lankcombe Ford *(7)*, and the walker should now make for the prominent signpost on the skyline to the north, and take the track signposted 'Malmsmead'.

After ½ mile (805 m) or so, at the junction of three tracks, take the L option, and shortly after, L again. Another ford is crossed and the track now leads to the tarmac road about ½ mile (805 m) ahead. Turn R down Post Lane, and Malmsmead is reached in ⅓ mile (535 m).

1 *Malmsmead*

It is here that Jan Ridd brought his bride Lorna, in R. D. Blackmore's celebrated novel *Lorna Doone*. The narrow bridge, the ford, the many horse riders and the red-roofed, whitewashed building now known as Lorna Doone Farm all create an unforgettable image. The Malmsmead Natural History Centre is open midweek in the summer. Shop, café, camp-site and lavatories.

2 *Cloud Farm*

The original house is almost lost among the jumble of stable extensions. The abutments of the old bridge—swept away in the great flood disaster which occurred in 1952—can be seen 25 yards (22 m) upstream from the present footbridge. The Badgworthy Water forms the county boundary between Devon to the west, and Somerset to the east.

3 *The Blackmore Memorial*

A stone beside the path reads:

To the memory of
Richard Doddridge Blackmore
whose novel LORNA DOONE
extols to all the world the
joys of Exmoor.

This stone was placed here by the Lorna Doone
Centenary Committee 1969

4 *Lank Combe*

The 'slide of water' mentioned by Blackmore is thought to

Badgworthy Water, near Blackmore memorial stone.

have been the one which may be seen up this side valley, but we must remember that *Lorna Doone* is a work of fiction.

5 *The Deer Park*
This was kept as a special reserve for the red deer by Nicholas Snow senior and junior in the last century.

6 *Medieval village site and the ruins of the shepherd's cottage*
The mounds beside the track at the eastern approach to Hoccombe Combe from Badgworthy Water represent a ruined settlement, deserted by 1400. They were woven into his novel *Lorna Doone* by Blackmore as the 'cots' of the Doones. The shepherd's cottage to the west was a much later building, and had a relatively short life.

7 *Lank Combe/Land Combe Hoccombe Combe/Hoccombe Water*
These two pairs of similar names represent different features in the area.

1.17

DICKY'S PATH AND DUNKERY BEACON

STARTING AND FINISHING
POINT
Webber's Post car-park (181-
903438).
LENGTH
6 miles (9½ km)
ASCENT
1000 ft (303 m)

An open moor walk in two parts. Most of the first half uses Dicky's Path which passes along the northern slopes of Dunkery Beacon just above the tree line. The second half traces the high ridge of the Rowbarrows, Dunkery Beacon, Kit Barrows and Joaney and Robin How. As this is a high-level walk a day of good visibility is recommended. This walk is entirely on land owned by the National Trust as part of the Holnicote (pronounced 'Hunnicut') Estate *(1)*.

ROUTE DESCRIPTION (Map 28)

From the informal National Trust car-park at Webber's Post *(2)*, walk uphill beside the Dunkery Beacon road—the more easterly of the two minor roads which converge here—to a point 100 yards (91 m) beyond the double bend where on the R (west) of the road is a PFS marked 'Dicky's Path to Stoke Pero' *(3)*.

This delectable route undulates beguilingly westwards across the northern skirts of the Dunkery massif, and is well marked and used, so yard by yard route instructions are unnecessary. In one's progress from east to west the minor valleys of Hollow Combe, Aller Combe, Sweetworthy Combe and Bagley Combe are encountered, each with their own little stream. Between Aller Combe and Sweetworthy Combe the walker will come across two fenced-off ancient monuments, and there is another beyond the beech hedge on the lower side *(4)*.

This is a good walk to observe birds as the path is constantly entering woods and leaving them for more open country. The habitats are therefore frequently changing *(5)*. Views to the north across the rolling tree-clad hills towards the Bristol Channel are best seen in late October or early November when the leaves are turning.

Immediately after crossing the small stream which flows down Bagley Combe—the fourth small valley since leaving the

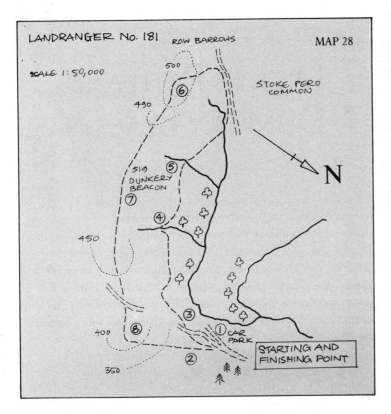

LANDRANGER No. 181   ROW BARROWS   MAP 28

SCALE 1:50,000

STOKE PERO COMMON

N

STARTING AND FINISHING POINT

CAR PARK

road—turn up a path L by a single Scots pine tree, and walk slanting uphill towards the road. When nearly at the road follow it up parallel with it and to the east. Where the path meets a National Trust informal pull-in beside a bend in the road, take the broad track heading south-east to the summit of Rowbarrows *(6)*. From here a broad path leads due east to Dunkery Beacon exactly 1 mile (1.6 km) away *(7)*. Now walk slightly north of east to the twin cairns of Kit Barrows, the next high ground further on, and from here descend to the road and continue north-east to the prominent cairn-bearing spur of Robin How and Joaney How *(8)*.

Walk north, downhill, for 50 yards (45 m) or so, and Webber's Post with its scattering of cars becomes visible due north and in line with Porlock.

1 The Holnicote Estate

The 12,420 acres (5,030 hectares) of the Holnicote Estate were given to the National Trust in 1944 by Sir Richard Acland, and extend from the sea to well south and west of Dunkery Beacon.

2 Webber's Post

A kind of breathing space on the steep road up from Horner and Luccombe where it divides. One branch twists its way to

Following page: *Sweetworthy Combe.*

Dunkery Beacon, Exmoor's highest point.

Cloutsham and Stoke Pero and the other climbs to the shoulder of Dunkery Beacon. The place is named after Tom Webber, a well-known staghunter in the last century.

3 *Dicky's Path*
This may have been named on Sir Richard Acland's 21st birthday in 1927, but is likely to be much older. It was the custom of the Acland family to name walks and rides after people, animals and events. See also the 'Horner Valley and Stoke Pero' walk (page 140).

4 *Settlement sites*
The Sweetworthy settlement sites are little understood. No excavation has been carried out, but it is presumed they belong to the Iron Age.

5 *Bird life*
Some of the birds seen along here are the green woodpecker, redstart, stonechat, buzzard and kestrel.

6 *Rowbarrows*
Exmoor's second highest point (after Dunkery Beacon) at 1674 feet (510 m). Several large Bronze Age cairns survive. The track along this watershed is probably an ancient one.

7 *Dunkery Beacon*
Exmoor's highest point at 1704 feet (520 m). A toposcope provided by the AA indicates the chief places seen on a clear day. The suffix 'Beacon' points to its use in early times as a fire signal station.

8 *Robin How and Joaney How*
'How' is Norse for a barrow, and there are actually three close together, and others on the hill slope. Robin and Joaney seem to be nineteenth-century names.

1.18

THE HORNER VALLEY
AND STOKE PERO

STARTING AND FINISHING
POINT
National Trust car-park at Horner
(181-897455).
LENGTH
6 miles (9½ km)
ASCENT
1600 ft (490 m)

A sheltered walk through one of Exmoor's finest wooded valleys, entirely in the National Trust's Holnicote (pronounced 'Hunnicut') Estate. The isolated church at Stoke Pero is visited, and the return leg of the excursion is more open, with fine views to Porlock Bay.

ROUTE DESCRIPTION (Map 29)

Leave the car-park at Horner by the way you drove in, turn L, and after 35 yards (32 m) turn R along a short path and cross a narrow stone packhorse bridge over the Horner Water *(1)*. Turn R, and L after 10 yards (9 m) up a steeply climbing path known as Cat's Scramble *(2)* which soon ascends more gently. The woods are initially of oak and beech with an under-storey of holly, and are sufficiently open for bracken to grow. The path, still gradually rising, passes round a small combe with views across to the return path across the valley. From here on the beech trees are absent. Where a path crosses Cat's Scramble go straight ahead *(3)*.

After passing round a second small combe, the path climbs to a patch of old coppice woodland *(4)*. The nests of wood ants are prominent here. At the top of a spur, ignore paths to the L and R and carry straight on. The path descends slightly, bearing R, then ascends again. Here the character of the woodland changes. The oaks are deformed and contorted *(5)*. A path comes in from the R, but may be ignored, and shortly after at an X junction bear L along the contours instead of carrying on uphill. This is Granny's Ride, and should be followed for some distance. Shortly after passing the site of some isolated storm damage a signposted cross path is met. Continue along Granny's Ride. The path narrows and drops steeply to a forestry track. Use this track to carry on down to the Horner Water which should be crossed by a footbridge.

A PFS on the R (south) bank indicates 'Stoke Pero' and this

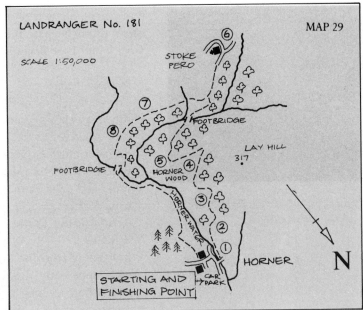

path should now be followed uphill. A path going off to the L 150 yards (137 m) from the bottom should be ignored, likewise another PFS near the top indicates the return route, and can be ignored for the present. The path enters a field and passes into a lane which is followed to a road by a small farm. This is Stoke Pero, and the farm is the only habitation near the church which is 50 yards (45 m) up the road *(6)*.

Return to the PFS in the woods, and take the path R marked 'Webber's Post' ignoring a gate straight ahead. Go steeply down for a short distance, ignoring a path going straight on and turn up R beyond a stream head. At a path junction in a dip, ignore the path going L and continue to follow the straight ahead path. It now emerges from the woods onto a bracken slope and levels out by a seat and some specimen conifers at Cloutsham Ball *(7)*. This is a fine viewpoint.

Beyond the seat take the R path at a fork. At a T-junction, turn L. A deep valley is in front down which flows the East Water. As you descend look out for large pollarded oaks *(8)*. Rejoin the other path, and at once there is another path junction. Follow the Nature Trail signs R. The path descends steeply, and the stream should be crossed by a footbridge.

Now take the path going downstream on the R bank, ignoring a steep path climbing to Webber's Post. At Nature Trail marker no. 7 take the path signposted 'Windsor Walk to Horner'. At cross paths, carry on contouring. Just beyond a signpost reading 'Webber's Post and Windsor Path' another signpost is found in the Scots pines pointing to 'Horner'. Go

Previous page and above: *Horner Water . . . a rich and varied habitat.*

down here, along a pleasant open path. The path gets steeper, passes through a gate and reaches the road just south of Horner. Turn L and the village is soon reached.

1 *Packhorse bridge*
There are several of these narrow, humped-backed bridges in the area. They are probably not more than 250 years old.

2 *Cat's Scramble*
As mentioned in Note 3 to the 'Dicky's Path and Dunkery Beacon' walk, the Acland family gave names to some of the walks and rides on their estate. Cat's Scramble may have been named after an agile pony called 'the Cat' ridden by Lady Acland in the 1870s.

3 *Holed oak*
Just before reaching this path junction look L to see the oak with, apparently, a large hole through the trunk. It is likely that, when a young tree, two branches fused together.

4 *Coppice woodland*
Coppicing is a form of woodland management rarely practised in the late twentieth century. At intervals of between ten and twenty years—depending on the market, the need for a cash crop, and the size of timber required—the trees were cut to within 1 foot (½ m) of the ground, and the material sold for a variety of purposes: pit props, fencing, firewood, charcoal and bark for tanning.

5 *Deformed oaks*
These trees are probably contorted as they are on a hillside exposed to the south-west wind. As young trees their twigs were repeatedly torn off and their trunks buffetted by gales.

6 *Stoke Pero church*
The highest church on Exmoor at 1013 feet (307 m). One building, Church Farm, shares its lonely position, but just over 100 years ago twelve cottages stood nearby. Ten farms are scattered around the far-flung parish. The church was rebuilt in 1897, and inside the building is a photograph of Zulu, the donkey which pulled the timber for the new roof up from Porlock.

7 *Cloutsham Ball*
The specimen conifers were planted by the Aclands in the last century.

8 *Pollarded oaks*
Like coppicing (see Note 4 above) pollarding was a system of woodland management rarely practised now. Trees were cut back to within several feet of ground level, probably above the browse-line of red deer, and the branches used for a variety of purposes. The resulting tree is known as a pollard.

2.19

Selworthy and Hurlstone Point

STARTING AND FINISHING
POINT
Selworthy church car-park (181-
920467).
LENGTH
6½ miles (10.4 km)
ASCENT
1500 ft (457 m)

A walk through unusual woods to the rugged promontory of Hurlstone Point, returning over the breezy eminence of Selworthy Beacon and past the Iron Age hill fort of Bury Castle.

Route Description (Map 30)

Leave the car-park and enter Selworthy Green *(1)* to the west of the church. Go down the path, and 5 yards (4.5 m) past the National Trust shop and information office turn R over a small stone footbridge signposted 'Bossington Hurlstone' into woods. After 20 yards (18 m) turn L over a stile and bear L ignoring a path going up R. After 250 yards (228.5 m) ignore a path going down to the L. A further 150 yards (137 m) on a cross path is met, but the correct route is to continue contouring. The path now runs along the edge of woods at the top of several fields, and a good view opens up to the south.

At a fork Catherine's Well (or Katherine's Well) appears on the R *(2)*. Bear L, still keeping along the top of fields. At Holnicote Combe, continue to contour, ignoring paths up and down to R and L, and the way is now along a broad track. At the next signposted cross path continue to contour following the 'Bossington' PFS.

When you reach a timber-loading area, take the lower of three facing tracks signposted 'Agnes Fountain Bossington'. This is Allerford Combe. Arriving at Agnes Fountain *(3)* one finds six paths meet at this spot, and there is a seat. Take the centre path heading north signposted 'Hurlstone Point Lower Path'. From here on the route will pass through extensive groves of ilex trees *(4)*. A path comes up from the L to join our track, and 100 yards (91 m) further on a path descending on the L can be ignored. At Lynch Combe the route goes through a gate and crosses an up and down path. Carry on through another gate signposted 'Hurlstone Point'. There are more ilex here. Yet another gate is entered in Church Combe, and there is a good example of

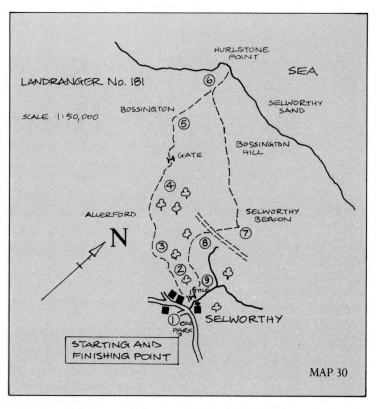

walling on the L, and the woods are left behind. A path goes down L to Bossington.

A good view is now seen *(5)*. As the route bears round to the R the view changes, and some scree slopes will be noticed. The foot of Hurlstone Combe is crossed—our return route—and a path is met coming up from the beach. A narrow path climbs to the rocky tip of Hurlstone Point where there is a coastguard lookout *(6)*. Once round the corner the path degenerates, so walkers are recommended to return when they have had a look. Landslips sweep the area and smooth grassy slopes at 45° make for dangerous walking.

Retrace your steps to the foot of Hurlstone Combe and walk up this dry valley. This is a long slog, but is not excessively steep. At the top, continue up the spur ignoring paths to the L and R and following the signpost 'Coast Path Minehead'. After 200 yards (182.8 m) a wartime track is met and this should be followed. A cairn is seen on Bossington Hill to the R. 30 yards (27.4 m) beyond a PFS pointing R and saying 'Lynch Combe' bear L at a fork. Here Selworthy Beacon comes into view ahead, and should be aimed for. There are fields on your L. At the summit of Selworthy Beacon *(7)* the view should be appreciated before leaving this elevated spot.

Descend by the track which approaches the summit at 45° to

Allerford Bridge.

the south from our own approach from the west. This track leads to an open glade of pine trees. The earthworks of Bury Castle—soon to be visited—are visible to the left at the edge of open land. The stone memorial hut *(8)* near the road should be seen, then the path through the trees followed by Bury Castle *(9)*. This earthwork bears a sign 'Bury Castle Iron Age Fort', and from this notice a path descends steeply, enters woods, and zigzags over a stile and down through the woods. Turn L at the main path and walk steeply down to a five-bar gate and a footbridge over a stream. 5 yards (4.5 m) beyond, climb the stile beside the stream. Recross it, and 10 yards (9 m) beyond you rejoin the outward path. Recross the stream for the last time and you are on Selworthy Green.

1 Selworthy church and Green

The white-walled church, so boldly placed on the south-facing hillside, is a landmark from many viewpoints. Conversely, the panorama from the church steps is unsurpassed in Somerset. Within, the features to look for are the window tracery, the richly-decorated wagon roof in the south aisle, carved bench ends, and fifteenth-century pulpit with sounding board and hour glass.

The thatched cottages round Selworthy Green were built

in 1828 to accommodate estate pensioners who were kitted out in red cloaks. The inspiration for the contrived appearance of cottages round a green was Blaise Hamlet, on the outskirts of Bristol, also now in the care of the National Trust. One of the cottages is now a small National Trust shop and another serves teas in the summer. There are lavatories at the foot of the Green.

2 *Katherine's Well*

A natural spring probably named after St Katherine or St Catherine, and thought to have special properties.

3 *Agnes Fountain*

Like Katherine's Well, a spring, probably named after St Agnes.

4 *Ilex trees*

The extensive groves of evergreen oak (*Quercus ilex*) were originally planted in 1815. It is unusual to find so many together. The ground beneath, being so shaded by year-round heavy green leaves, is devoid of weed growth.

5 *The view*

The low-lying land is the highly fertile Vale of Porlock. Porlock Weir is at the far end and beyond are the wooded slopes of Culbone and Glenthorne trailing off to the Foreland in the distance. Porlock is to the L and the round chimneys of Bossington can be seen below.

Left: *A prehistoric cairn (right) on the summit of Selworthy Beacon.*

Above: *Bury Castle.*

6 *Hurlstone Point*

This rugged promontory has also been called Hurststone, Hustone and Huntstone Point. The coastguard lookout has been boldly embellished with the stone walls and small turrets of a castle.

7 *Selworthy Beacon*

At 1012 feet (308 m) the highest point on this detached piece of Exmoor. Like Dunkery Beacon, it was used as a fire signal station in times of emergency during medieval times.

8 *Stone memorial hut*

Sometimes known as the 'wind and weather hut', this is a memorial to the 10th Baronet, Sir Thomas Dyke Acland (1787–1871). He was fond of walking this way on Sundays, and some of the quotations with which he entertained his family are inscribed in the hut.

9 *Bury Castle*

An Iron Age earthwork where defences employed the tip of a spur above Selworthy.

2.20

WATERSMEET

STARTING AND FINISHING POINT
National Trust car-park and picnic site just inside the Combe Park Hotel grounds, near Hillsford Bridge (180-740477).

LENGTH
7 miles (11.2 km)

ASCENT
1200 ft (365.7 m)

A figure-of-eight walk to discover the wooded valleys and breezy uplands of the National Trust's Watersmeet Estate. There are several opportunities for refreshments 'in the season'.

ROUTE DESCRIPTION (Map 31)

Leave the car-park and picnic site by heading for Hillsford Bridge, and walk up the grass verge beside the A39 behind the AA point. Where it tapers, keep to the road edge and make for the National Trust sign 'Watersmeet' 50 yards (45.7 m) ahead. Pass up a pleasant grassy track and enter a gate. These are beautiful, mostly oak, woods, and like so much of the valley woodlands of Exmoor were once managed on the coppice system *(1)*.

Where the path levels out a beautiful view unfolds. Spurs and valleys are complicatedly interwoven. Ignore a PFS by a seat pointing to 'Watersmeet', and carry on, likewise ignoring a PFS pointing L to 'East Lyn'. The views now encompass Lynton and Lynmouth with the Bristol Channel beyond. At an acute path

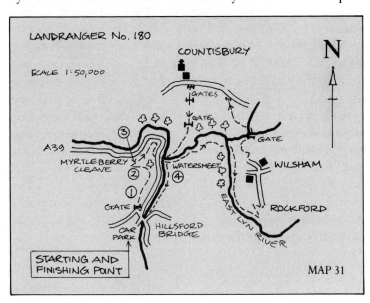

junction R, descend the steep path heading for Watersmeet. Note Butter Hill and Countisbury church *(2)* on the hilltop ahead before losing height. An Iron Age earthwork will be passed through on the open ground before re-entering the woodland *(3)*, then the path hurries down to the road, the A39, which must be crossed to the small National Trust staff car-park opposite. Do exercise care here, as the crossing is on a corner which is almost blind for traffic coming up the road.

The path descends to Watersmeet. Cross the first of two footbridges, over the Hoar Oak Water, but turn up the riverbank of the second river, the East Lyn, instead of crossing the second footbridge *(4)*.

So, walk up the L bank of the East Lyn river, passing the gaping mouth of a short mining adit after a few yards *(5)*. About 400 yards (364 m) upstream are the restored remains of a lime kiln *(6)* with a small quarry nearby. Another 400 yards (364 m) or so upstream take the L fork at a path junction, and cross Ash Bridge when you reach it *(7)*. Turn R on the R bank, and walk up the valley for about 1 mile (1.6 km). Opposite Rockford Cottage—a small café—turn up L at a PFS 'Wilsham Countisbury'. The path zigzags up and turns L along a walled track. The path is waymarked with yellow paint. At Wilsham keep the house with four dormers on your L and follow a broad grassy track northwards.

At an iron gate, turn half R, go down and up into a combe. The path slants up and around a moorland slope and reaches the A39 by an iron gate. Turn L along this busy road, exercising great care, for about 300 yards (274.3 m) when you should turn L into a lane signposted 'Watersmeet'. (This is just behind the Exmoor Sandpiper Inn, formerly the Blue Ball Inn and the Blue Boar Inn.

Follow this gated lane, entering a field at the end and keeping about 25 yards (22.8 m) from the L hedge and aiming for a spur ahead. Note the opposite hillside; this was traversed earlier in the walk. The foot of the field is vacated by a hunting gate, and here there is a PFS sign pointing four ways, and a seat. Go straight ahead, along an attractive grassy spur. The path heading for 'Countisbury' is Winston's Path *(8)*. The path drops off the end of the spur down through the woods, and after the second hairpin bend look out for a sign R marked 'Viewpoint only'. This goes about 45 yards (41 m) through the trees to the top of a rocky buttress overlooking the East Lyn, but do not leave the path or take risks as the drop is considerable.

East Lyn river and Watersmeet House.

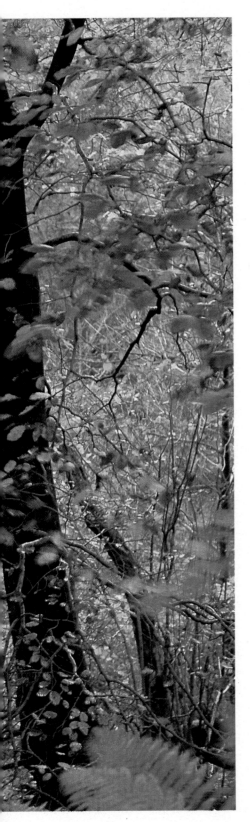

The downhill path reaches the riverside just upstream from Watersmeet House—another refreshment chance. Cross the East Lyn, but instead of going over the Hoar Oak Water, ascend the steps opposite the National Trust money box, turn R at the top signposted 'Hillsford Bridge' and follow the path up to Hillsford Bridge. Do however look out for a short path heading down to the Hoar Oak Water R after 300 yards (274.3 m) from the top of the steps. This leads to a two-stage waterfall viewpoint, and photographers will find it worth seeing.

At Hillsford Bridge, cross the road, cross the bridge, and turn L into the car-park.

1 *Coppice woodland*
See Note 4 of 'The Horner Valley and Stoke Pero' walk (page 140).

2 *Butter Hill and Countisbury*
See Notes 1 and 2 of the 'Countisbury to County Gate' walk (pages 155–7).

3 *Myrtleberry North earthworks*
A univallate (one-banked) enclosure of about 1 acre (0.4 hectares) with an outwork to the south-west.

4 *Watersmeet House*
Built by the Halliday family about 1830 as a fishing and shooting lodge, it now accommodates a National Trust café and shop. There are lavatories round the back.

5 *Mining adit*
An attempt to find iron ore. An adit is a horizontal shaft. Not much ore was found, hence the short tunnel.

6 *Lime kiln and quarry*
The local soil is acid, but could be sweetened by the addition of lime. Limestone was brought to Lynmouth from South Wales by coasting craft and brought up here by packhorses. Locally-produced charcoal was used in the firing. The small quarry is where the stone came from to build Watersmeet House.

7 *Ash Bridge*
This bridge was built in 1983 by a Manpower Services Commission team.

8 *Winston's Path*
This path is named after Winston Singleton, the National Trust warden who created it.

Watersmeet—leaf, light and water.

2.21

COUNTISBURY TO
COUNTY GATE

STARTING AND FINISHING POINT
National Trust car-park at Countisbury (180-747496).
LENGTH
8 miles (12.8 km)
ASCENT
1700 ft (518 m)

A coastal walk along the little-known cliffs between the Foreland and Glenthorne, returning over high ground. Good views across the Bristol Channel to Wales.

ROUTE DESCRIPTION (Map 32)

Leave the car-park by the gate in the upper wall, turn L and enter the churchyard. Visit the church if desired *(1)*. Pass round the west end of the church, and leave the churchyard by the stile in the north wall. You are now on the open cliff top.

Head half R for 100 yards (91.4 m) to a PFS and continue uphill to the prominent mast and small building on the summit of Butter Hill *(2)*. Walk due north from the summit making for the fenced wall which soon comes into view R. The path steepens and reaches the coast path at a railed-off landslide called Great Red. Carry on north for 150 yards (137 m), but in a saddle, a signpost advises a R turn along the coast path. (The direct path is not maintained and the public use it at their own risk. The slopes away from the true path are precarious and rather hairy to use.) The path descends the side of a steep dry valley with acres of scree slopes, itself a satellite of the larger Caddow Combe to which the path leads, and down which the lighthouse road passes. As you reach the lighthouse road the scree/heather/bracken hill ahead is Warmersturt. (Here a diversion down the road may be made to the lighthouse, and ¼ mile (1.2 km) /¼ hour should be added to the route *(3)*.)

Turn R up the straight stretch of road, bearing L at the first hairpin bend—the road is private, and frighteningly steep to drive over—along a track signposted 'Coast Path'. The possibility of climbing Warmersturt to your L signposted as 'Viewpoint' does not add much to the splendid view experienced from the track as it passes over the shoulder ahead *(4)*. Pass over the stile beside the gate leading to Rodney Cottage, a very remote dwelling, and climb a few steps to the

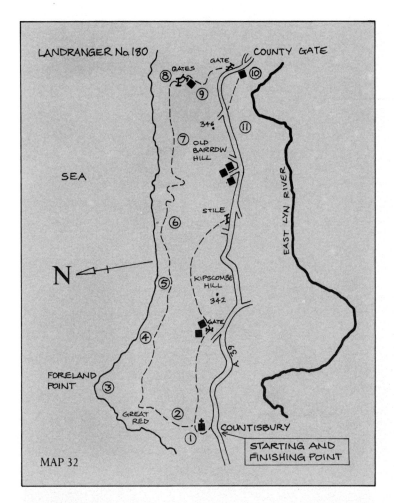

LANDRANGER No 180

GATE

COUNTY GATE

⑧ GATES

⑩

⑨

346

⑪

⑦ OLD BARROW HILL

SEA

STILE

⑥

EAST LYN RIVER

N

⑤

KIPSCOMBE HILL

342

⑥

④

GATE

FORELAND POINT

A 39

③

GREAT RED

②

COUNTISBURY

①

STARTING AND FINISHING POINT

MAP 32

coast path. A National Trust sign announces 'Glenthorne Cliffs'. At the first seat along the path look back to see the end of the lighthouse road and the agitated sea off the Foreland. The lighthouse itself is invisible, being tucked away into the cliff slope. The path enters pleasant open mixed woodland. There is no trace of Rodney Cottage, but the sound of poultry may reach the walker.

The route enters and leaves several small combes, each with its tiny stream, though they do dry up in drought conditions. Chub Hill Combe is followed by Swannel Combe. Beyond here some rhododendron patches have been eradicated. This is fairy woodland, lacking recent management, but some trees were pollarded in the past *(5)*. Look out particularly for a large tree on the higher side of the path 150 yards (137 m) west of Pudleep Girt which is in the process of 'swallowing up' a large boulder.

About 200 yards (182.8 m) east of Pudleep Girt a sign warns 'Path closed due to cliff fall', so the bypass path loops

strenuously up and round the landslip, passing a ruined estate folly on the R *(6)*. The path levels out, then drops to meet the true route beyond the landslip. The route now loops round Dogsworthy Combe and Wingate Combe while contouring the slopes. Beyond Wingate Combe take the higher path option at a fork signposted 'Culbone, County Gate'. The route passes (1987) through a tunnel of rhododendrons. (They could be eradicated, as they are a weed species.) Look out on the R for a small walled seat shelter, and 100 yards (91.4 m) further on a stone seat. A stone wall is passed, and a further stone seat *(7)*.

The path meets the Glenthorne drive *(8)* and the walker should turn R signposted 'Culbone'. Walk past 'The Lodge', and once past the twin boars' head gateposts, the Halliday armorial beasts, turn down L signposted 'Culbone'. Pass through two small gates, past the Sisters' Fountain *(9)* and climb 10 yards (9 m) up to an estate drive. Turn R up here signposted 'County Gate' and 100 yards (91.4 m) further on turn L at Seven Thorns, again signposted 'County Gate'. This is a steep climb to the A39.

Arriving at the main road, follow it for 10 yards (9 m) then cross the road to the viewpoint car-park at County Gate *(10)*. From the west end of the car-park take the footpath over Cosgate Hill. Descend the west side of the hill to a small car-park noting as you go the top end of Glenthorne drive to your R, with its own letter box. The Roman fortlet of Old Burrow *(11)* will also be seen in the field beyond. Now walk on the wide grass verge on the south side of the A39 for about ¼ mile (1.2 km) to a stile on the north side near Dogsworthy Cottage. This path, which passes through a number of fields, is signposted 'Countisbury', and is waymarked with yellow paint. Keep the field wall on your R and make for the fence in the far corner. Enter the gate, but keep the wall on your R. Carry on past gate 'To Desolate'. The next gate is 30 yards (27.4 m) away from the wall. Now contour across the field, aiming for the Butter Hill mast in the distance and making for the stile in a non-existent fence.

50 yards (45.7 m) on a gate becomes visible carrying a yellow waymark. Enter here, following the lower edge of the field to another waymarked gate. Follow the field edge past a round-roofed barn, across the farm approach road, and follow a field hedge to a gate on the lighthouse road. Cross the road, and follow the track, taking a L fork after 25 yards (22.8 m). Keep on the main track, bearing slightly L to a PFS by the wall. Keep the wall on your L and follow it to Countisbury.

1 Countisbury church

The church is more remarkable for its situation than for its

Opposite: The Foreland from Countisbury Hill.

appearance and contents. However the north aisle has high-backed pews, and there is an unusual classical pediment in the chancel arch.

2 *Butter Hill*

Butter Hill rises to 993 feet, and is crowned by a long-disused signal station, now adapted to modern communications. A television mast and relay station boosts reception down to Lynton and Lynmouth, and there is shelter for walkers.

3 *The Foreland*

The Foreland is the northernmost tip of Devon, and is owned by the National Trust. The lighthouse was built in 1900.

4 *The view east*

You are looking along the Glenthorne Cliffs to Culbone, with Hurlstone Point in the distance. This is a lonely coastline, with no road access until Porlock Weir is reached.

5 *Pollarded trees*

See Note 8 on pollarded trees in 'The Horner Valley and Stoke Pero' walk (page 140).

6 *Ruined folly*

Nothing is known about this little building, but it is likely to have been constructed in the last century by the Hallidays of Glenthorne as a shelter during their coastal walks.

7 *Stone seats*

These were provided by the Hallidays for themselves and their guests when out walking.

8 *The Glenthorne Drive*

When Glenthorne House was built in 1832 by the Revd W. Halliday near sea level he had first to build the drive which was started in 1829, and took a year to construct. It is 3 miles (5 km) long and drops 950 feet (288 m).

9 *The Sisters' Fountain*

A cross surmounting a spring, named after the four sisters who were nieces of the Revd W. Halliday, who built Glenthorne House.

10 *County Gate*

County Gate Cottage, which stands beside the boundary of Devon and Somerset, is now a summer-only Exmoor National Park information centre. It was once known as the Road House and provided refreshment for the few travellers along this lonely road.

11 *Old Burrow* (not Old Barrow as shown on the OS map)

The Roman fortlet or signal station was occupied only briefly, from AD 48 to 52. It was probably too elevated to be of much use, mist would have frequently obscured the view, so it was succeeded by a similar construction at a slightly lower altitude between Heddon's Mouth and Woody Bay.

Opposite: *Looking east from County Gate.*

157

3.22

WOODY BAY TO HOLDSTONE DOWN

STARTING AND FINISHING
POINT
Woody Bay National Trust car-park
(180-676486).
LENGTH
14 miles (22.5 km)
ASCENT
2000 ft (609.5 m)

A largely coastal walk exploiting the great variety of Exmoor scenery, and particularly the unspoilt country where the moor meets the sea.

ROUTE DESCRIPTION (Map 33)

From the roadside car-park above Woody Bay *(1)*, walk up to the first hairpin bend and enter a gate facing you signposted 'Coast Path'. This is a well-engineered track with no severe ups and downs for nearly 3 miles (4.8 km). After 50 yds (45.7 m) a seat marks a fine viewpoint *(2)*.

Round the first left-hand bend a view opens up ahead, and the return path can be seen further down the cliff side.

After walking for about 1½ miles (2.4 km) the track veers L into and above the great coastal indentation known as the Heddon Valley *(3)*. The track continues easily downwards to the Hunters' Inn, the last ½ mile (805 m) being through woods, and at the bottom there are opportunities for refreshment.

From the inn take the road signposted 'Combe Martin, Barnstaple' for about 300 yds (274.3 m) and just before the bridge take the signposted track L which follows the river upstream. After 400 yds (365.7 m) at a farm track junction, turn down sharp R signposted 'Trentishoe Mill', cross a footbridge by a cottage, turn L and follow the track up the valley, taking the L fork at the next junction, again signposted 'Trentishoe Mill'.

A path comes in from the L and our route meets and follows a minor road coming down from the R. Carry on along here ignoring a path going up 10 yds (9 m) further on signposted 'Trentishoe Down & Ladies Mile'. At the entrance to Trentishoe Manor turn R along the path marked 'Ladies Mile', and after 150 yds (137 m) turn up sharp L. The path is waymarked with yellow-topped posts and leads to a broad track which gradually becomes more open and reaches the road over Trentishoe

Down near the Moorlands Tea Rooms (summer only, not Sundays) where there are a few houses *(4)*.

Take the track going up beside Moorlands leading to the summit of Holdstone Down *(5)*. Carry on down the west side of Holdstone Down in line with the top of the Great Hangman, the bulky hill beyond the deep ravine of Sherry Combe *(6)*. Where the coast path is met, here passing L to R, turn R and follow the path round. When the houses on Trentishoe Down come into view, bear L off the track and follow a narrow path making for a stile in the west edge of the fields in front of you.

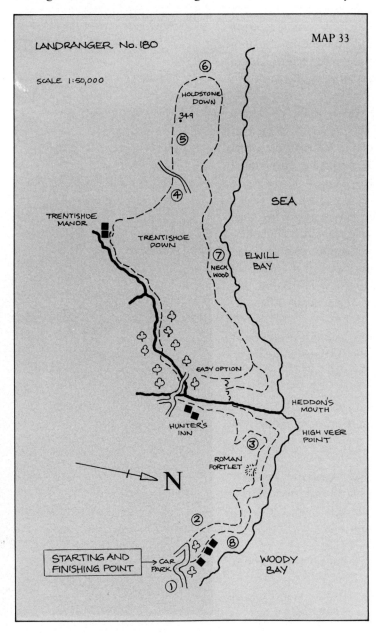

. . . in the Heddon Valley.

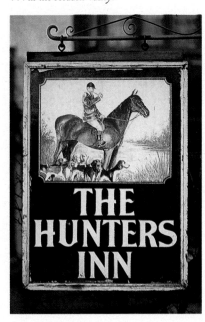

Enter the field, follow the path to the stile opposite, noting the precariously-sited trees of Neck Wood below *(7)*. The path now follows the outside of the enclosure walls, except at Bosley Gut, where the walker has to cross two stiles to circumvent a landslip.

Just before the path turns R along the top west side of the Heddon Valley, a newish, rough and somewhat scarey track goes down and around Peter Rock, rejoining the zig-zag path a little way down.

At the zig-zag, which can be reached if desired by carrying on along the top path instead of opting for the rough path, turn L—down—and L at the bottom. Take the first turning R, cross the river by a sturdy bridge, turn L and take the first R up a pleasant slanting path leading towards Highveer Point. This is the lower path, some distance down the cliff from the track you used on the outward leg of the walk.

The path passes the waterfall at Hollow Brook Combe, a charming corner, goes into woods and is here very near the cliff edge. West Woody Bay Wood is entered *(8)* and the path meets the road descending to Woody Bay at a hairpin. Turn uphill here and the car-park is soon reached.

1 *Woody Bay*

About the turn of the century an entrepreneur tried to turn the inlet of Woody Bay into a second Lynmouth. He built a pier here—of which the concrete stump remains—and encouraged the Bristol Channel paddle steamers to call. A tea room provided teas. But he was charged with misdirecting clients' funds (he was a solicitor) and the scheme collapsed.

2 *Viewpoint*

The Valley of Rocks, just W of Lynton, can be picked out. A little further on from the seat the extensive rambling buildings of Lee Abbey, a religious retreat, will be seen.

3 *The Heddon Valley*

A wild cleavage in the coastline down which a path winds to the pebbly beach at Heddon's Mouth, where there is a limekiln.

4 *Trentishoe Down*

The few buildings here are all that remain of another grandiose development plan. The whole of Holdstone Down was split up into plots and offered for sale. Only a few, the ones near the road, were actually built on.

5 *Holdstone Down*

This lofty hill always seems to present a sinister aspect from a

The summit of Holdstone Down, with Great Hangman in the background.

Heddon's Mouth.

distance. It is designated a holy mountain by the Aetherius Society who hold meetings on its summit. Bronze Age barrows or cairns will be seen on its top.

6 *Sherry Combe*

A similar declivity to the Heddon Valley, but even wilder, and impossible to penetrate except by the coast path. Geologically it is a younger valley as it doesn't meet the sea at sea-level. A waterfall visible only from the sea drops its stream to the unwelcoming beach.

7 *Neck Wood*

A strange woodland survival on an incredibly steep north-facing slope. Its sheer inaccessibility has prevented its exploitation in the past.

8 *West Woody Bay Wood*

A large part of this wood was blown down in a blizzard in December 1981, but the replanted trees are beginning to assert themselves.

THE TWO MOORS WAY (EXMOOR SECTION)

STARTING AND FINISHING
POINT
Southern boundary of Exmoor
National Park–Badlake Moor Cross
(181-857284)
Footpath exit opposite St. John's
Church on A39, Lynmouth (180-
724494)
LENGTH
23 miles (35.4 km)
ASCENT
2500 ft (853.4 m)

An infinitely varied walk across the Exmoor National Park from south to north. The complete Two Moors Way extends south across mid-Devon, then over the Dartmoor National Park to Ivybridge, a total distance of 103 miles (165 km). This walk may be conveniently broken into a two-day stint at Blue Gate, where it crosses the Simonsbath to South Molton road.

ROUTE DESCRIPTION (Maps 34—36)

From Badlake Moor Cross take the rough rutted track going due north and slightly rising. Where it meets the ridge road running over East and West Anstey Commons carry on north with a beech hedge right for 1 mile (1.6 km). Turn L, downhill, at the next road.

This road descends steeply to cross the Dane's Brook at Slade Bridge *(1)*. Ascending the north side, at a sharp left-hand bend enter a field R to cut off a corner, passing an ash tree and making for a gate in the far corner of the field. Follow the road to the small village of Hawkridge, where you should turn L *(2)*.

After passing the last building on the R, enter a field, and walk diagonally across it, the first of five fields which are linked by gates or stiles. The last three fields are traced where the field meets the woods which here cover the valley side.

Where the path reaches a convergence of tracks, turn sharp R down a track signposted 'Tarr Steps Unfit for Motors' which soon reaches the riverside road at Penny Bridge. Turn L here, walking upstream, and Tarr Steps is soon reached *(3)*.

Cross this primitive bridge, and follow up the east bank. For the next 5½ miles (8.8 km), until the road is reached at Withypool, the path holds the same bank of the river Barle and no additional instructions *(4)* are necessary to add to the secure 'handrail' of the river on your L *(5)*.

At the road turn L and follow it through Withypool *(6)* turning up past the school, and following the red waymarks up

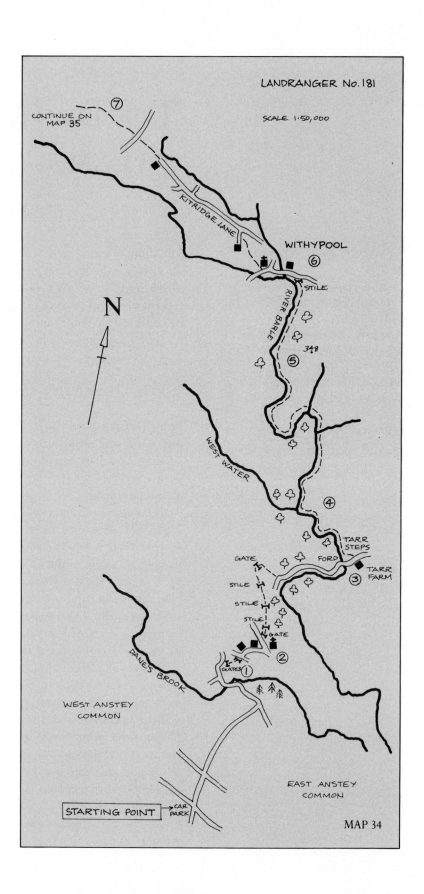

LANDRANGER No. 181

SCALE 1:50,000

CONTINUE ON
MAP 35

⑦

KITRIDGE LANE

WITHYPOOL ⑥

STILE

RIVER BARLE

N

348

⑤

WEST WATER

④

TARR
STEPS

GATE

FORD

TARR
FARM ③

STILE

STILE

STILE

GATE

②

GATES ①

DANE'S BROOK

WEST ANSTEY
COMMON

EAST ANSTEY
COMMON

STARTING POINT → CAR
PARK

MAP 34

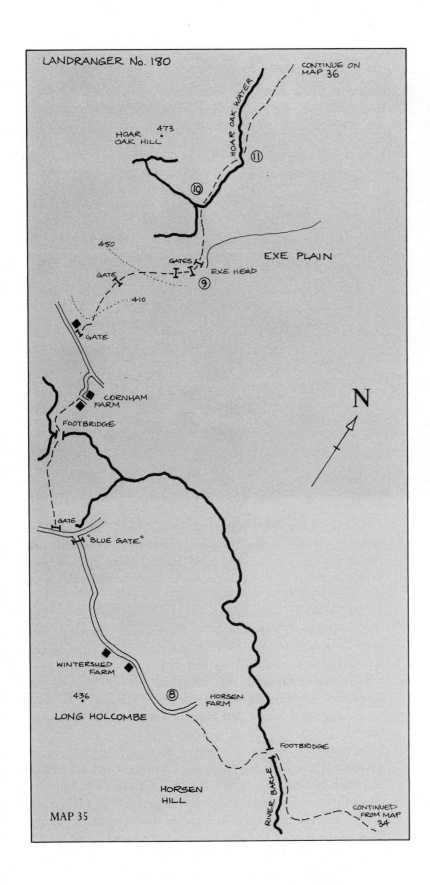

LANDRANGER No. 180

CONTINUE ON
MAP 36

HOAR OAK WATER

HOAR
OAK HILL
• 473

⑪

⑩

450

GATES

EXE PLAIN

GATE

EXE HEAD

⑨

410

GATE

N

CORNHAM
FARM

FOOTBRIDGE

GATE

"BLUE GATE"

WINTERSHED
FARM

• 436

⑧

HORSEN
FARM

LONG HOLCOMBE

FOOTBRIDGE

HORSEN
HILL

RIVER BARLE

CONTINUED
FROM MAP
34

MAP 35

Slade Bridge over Dane's Brook.

to Kitridge Lane. Turn L here and walk steadily upwards. The tarmac road ends where the track enters open moorland with enclosures on your L. The road leading down to Landacre Bridge is crossed and the track should continue to be followed, still with fields L.

The head of a small combe is circumnavigated (7) and the track signposted 'Simonsbath via Cow Castle' followed. This goes down and around, through an ancient wall, and up the river Barle to a conifer plantation.

Here the Barle should be crossed by a footbridge, and the signposted instruction 'Blue Gate 2½ miles' followed. The track is now clear and climbs past Horsen farm to a road leading to Blue Gate past Wintershed farm (8).

At Blue Gate, turn L and then R into the first gate. This is signposted 'Challacombe Road via Cornham Ford 1½ miles'. The track is initially level, but soon drops down a side valley to the Barle once more which is crossed by a footbridge. The path is clear beyond the bridge and climbs up to bypass Cornham farm on the west of its buildings, reaching the B3358 along the

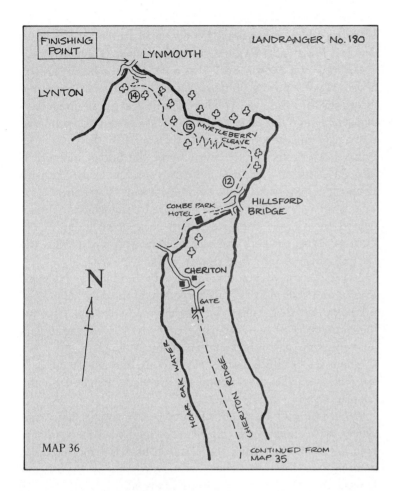

approach drive to the farm.

Turn L along what can be a busy road, facing oncoming traffic and walking in single file. At the second gate on the R, signposted 'Exe Head 1½ miles' leave the road and follow the red waymarks north bearing north-east after passing through a beech-lined hedge. Here the path is non-existent on the ground but a north-east direction should be followed, and if the top wall is met it can be followed along to the east to a succession of three gates which conduct the walker past the muddy puddles of Exe Head *(9)*. Here a signpost 'Hoar Oak' is useful.

Now head due north ignoring the headwaters of the Exe which trickle away easterly. Instead make for the cleavage of the Hoar Oak Water visible ahead and follow it down. A prominent round ruin—a sheepfold—stands on a rocky knoll at the foot of Long Chains Combe and may be visited *(10)*. Nearly ½ mile (0.8 km) further on a single tree will be noticed on the east bank growing inside a small fenced enclosure. This is the Hoar Oak Tree *(11)*.

Continue due north following a track along the spine of

Hawkridge Parish Church.

Cheriton Ridge and making for the small hamlet of Cheriton. The last few hundred yards are reached down a rough track.

Arriving at Cheriton, turn L at a PFS 'Lyncombe, Lyndown, Scoresdown' and almost immediately R at a fork signposted 'Scoresdown, Lyndown'. Follow this lane past Scoresdown farm and steeply into the valley of the Hoar Oak Water down a once-tarmaced but now heavily-rutted lane. At the foot Old Scoresdown nestles by the river. Cross the bridge and turn R into the National Trust Combe Park estate and take the path signposted 'Riverside Walk Combe Park 1 Watersmeet 1¼'. This is an easily followed and well-used path which loops up behind the Combe Park Hotel and back down again to the National Trust car park and picnic site at Hillsford Bridge, the starting point of the 'Watersmeet' walk.

Leave the car park and picnic site by heading for Hillsford Bridge, and walk up the grass verge beside the A39 behind the AA point. Where it tapers, keep to the road edge and make for the National Trust sign Watersmeet 50 yds (45.7 m) ahead. Pass up a pleasant grassy track and enter a gate.

These are beautiful, mostly oak, woods, and like so much of the valley woodlands of Exmoor were once managed on the coppice system *(12)*.

Where the path levels out a beautiful view unfolds. Spurs and valleys are complicatedly interwoven. Ignore a PFS by a seat pointing to 'Watersmeet', and carry on likewise ignoring a PFS pointing L to 'East Lyn'. The views now encompass Lynton and Lynmouth with the Bristol Channel beyond.

At an acute path junction R stay on the top path and carry on soon losing height down a zig-zag to negotiate a small side valley *(13)*. The path climbs the other side and soon an unsignposted path heads off L.

Turn down R where a PFS reads 'Lynmouth ¼'. This uses a well-contrived cutting through a rocky outcrop and soon meets another path coming in from the L from 'Lynbridge' (PFS).

The path carries on down through woodland and ends down a steep, walled path to reach the raised pavement beside the A39 opposite St. John's Church *(14)*.

1 *Slade Bridge*
   This marks the county boundary—Somerset to the north, Devon to the south. A parish boundary stone in the downstream parapet reads 'Hawkridge/West Anstey'.

2 *Hawkridge*
   There is a small Post Office here, and refreshments may be obtainable in the season.

3 *Tarr Steps*
   This stone causeway/bridge of seventeen spans is about 55

yds (50.3 m) long, and goes back to medieval times, though its primitive construction defies accurate dating. The bridge has several times been damaged by floods, so a cable debris-arrester is now positioned upstream to intercept floating logs which might damage the bridge. Refreshments are available here in the season, and lavatories are a few hundred yards up the approach road, in the public car park.

4 *Riverside path*

The Ordnance Survey 2½ in map shows the public right of way going from side to side of the river, crossing at unfordable fords, so the National Park Authority has negotiated a permissive path up the east bank.

5 *Deer*

Red deer are sometimes seen up this valley, particularly at the Withypool end.

6 *Withypool*

A good place for a rest. Here will be found a pub, café (in season), shop and public lavatories.

7 *Fox*

A fox was seen in this valley during the preparation of this book. Buzzards and the croaking raven may also be spotted.

8 *The Knights*

Horsen farm and Wintershed farm were both established by the innovative Knight family in the last century.

9 *Exe Head*

A very undramatic place for the headwaters of one of the West Country's major rivers. Exmouth is 55 miles (88.5 km) away.

10 *The Sheepfold*

A ruined cottage is incorporated into this interesting structure. A good place to hear the cuckoo.

11 *Hoar Oak Tree*

The present tree dates from 1917, and replaces one planted in 1662. It is an ancient boundary mark of the old Royal Forest or hunting ground, and stands on the county boundary too.

12 *Coppice woodland*

See note 4 of 'The Horner Valley and Stoke Pero'.

13 *Side Valley*

Although only a small combe, the descent is steep. At the bottom a ferny, tree-shaded stream tinkles down a fairy dell.

14 *Tow Moors Way stone*

A stone dated 29 May 1976 marks the northern end of the 103-mile walk.

Homesick . . .

APPENDICES

Access for the Walker

It is important to realize at the outset that the designation of a National Park does not change the ownership of land within it in any way. In the case of Dartmoor National Park in 1987 only 1.4 per cent of the land was actually owned by the National Park Authority, and only 25 per cent by all 'public' bodies (excluding the Duchy of Cornwall) combined, e.g. South West Water, the Forestry Commission, etc. The laws of access and trespass apply just as much to areas of private land within a National Park as to those outside it.

The National Parks and Access to the Countryside Act of 1949 required County Councils in England and Wales to prepare maps which showed all paths over which the public had a right to walk. The final form of the map is referred to as a Definitive Map and copies are held at the offices of the County Council and by Dartmoor and Exmoor Park Authorities. The inclusion of a public right of way on a definitive map can be taken as proof that such exists. Paths can only be diverted or deleted from a definitive map by the raising of a Diversion Order or an Extinguishment Order respectively. The paths are classified as either footpaths (for walkers only) or bridleways (for walkers, horse riders and cyclists). For definitive routes always use up-to-date maps. Public rights of way are included on the Ordnance Survey's 1:50,000 First and Second Series (i.e. Landranger), the 1:25,000 Second series (i.e. Pathfinder), and the Outdoor Leisure maps. On Dartmoor and Exmoor the rights of way network extends for some 1000 miles (1609 km) and the Park Authorities are responsible for all matters concerning the network. All these rights of way are well waymarked in both National Parks.

However, if this was the end of the matter, the right of access for the walker within the Dartmoor and Exmoor National Parks would be severely restricted. There are considerable areas of land without any public rights of way and sometimes the legal paths do not provide logical walking options. Fortunately, however, access to large areas is allowed in practice under one or more of the following:

THE DARTMOOR COMMONS ACT 1985:
Under this Act the public now has a legal right of access to all registered common land on Dartmoor—some 90,000 acres (36,423 ha). Such access is subject to certain byelaws to regulate public behaviour. Up to 1985, access to most of these commons was not 'legal' but was tolerated where public behaviour was sensible. This 'de facto' access situation—which still applies to large areas of common land outside the Dartmoor National Park—had existed for many years but did not confer any right of access upon the public.

Before the Act several means of securing access to this open country were pursued, either by Access Agreement or by Order; by National Park ownership such as Holne Moor and Haytor Down, or by declarations made by owners (or previous owners) under Section 193 of the 1925 Law of Property Act granting a public right of access 'for air and exercise', subject to byelaws, such as on Spitchwick Common in the Dartmeet and Newbridge areas.

TRADITION:
Walkers have for many years walked freely on most moorland areas of the National Parks. Some

large areas of moorland on Dartmoor are not legally registered as common and here traditional access still largely exists such as on parts of Walkhampton Common, and within the Ministry of Defence's Willsworthy Firing Range giving access to Tavy Cleave—but, in the case of the latter, access is obviously restricted when firing is in progress. Such 'de facto' access depends on the sensible behaviour of the walkers themselves.

Newtakes are not part of the commons. They may have similar vegetation, but they are enclosed. They form part of a freehold or, as in most cases, a tenancy for which rent is paid. In the larger and more remote newtakes, where no access agreements as yet exist or are considered unnecessary, owners and tenants generally tolerate access so long as no damage is done. Litter, broken glass, ruined walls, unruly dogs, noisy behaviour, etc. are likely to make it more difficult for the next people to go that way.

ACCESS AGREEMENTS:

Under the National Parks Access to the Countryside Act of 1949 and the Wildlife and Countryside Act 1981, the National Park Authorities are able to negotiate access agreements with landowners and tenants whereby access is given in return for compensation—either financial or in kind. Such access is subject to conditions as appropriate to the area; for example, access may be over all the land in question or may be restricted to defined routes. By the summer of 1987 some 17 access agreements had been concluded in the Dartmoor National Park providing new walking opportunities in some woods, newtakes and other areas. Most agreements also provide for the positive management of land for landscape and/or archaeological or wildlife conservation. Information boards have been provided at access entry points.

NATIONAL TRUST AREAS:

In 1987 the National Trust owned 13.8%, of the area of the Parks. The Trust's policy is to give free access, subject to byelaws, at all times to its open spaces such as the Plym Estate and Trowlesworthy Warren areas on Dartmoor. However, there cannot be unrestricted access to tenanted farms, young plantations and some woods, certain nature reserves where the conservation of fauna and flora is paramount, or on some country estates.

FORESTRY COMMISSION FORESTS:

The Forestry Commission manages, either by freehold or leasehold, some 4263 acres (1725 ha) of plantations on Dartmoor including Fernworthy, Bellever and Soussons. The Outdoor Leisure Map shows where forest trails and car parking has been provided. Please adhere to Forestry Commission byelaws in these areas and, in particular, guard against all risk of fire and do not approach men and machines at work.

SOUTH WEST WATER:

On Dartmoor, South West Water owns Venford, Burrator, Kennick, Tottiford, Trenchford, Meldon, Avon and Fernworthy Reservoirs. Walking opportunities exist around most of the reservoirs. The Water Authority also owns large moorland catchment areas, which serve these reservoirs, some of which are not registered common land; by tradition walkers have access onto these areas, but livestock graze here and it is important that dogs are kept under proper control and preferably on a lead during the lambing season. Currently, South West Water owns 8902 acres (3603 ha) on Dartmoor. Privatization of the Water Authorities is imminent and new landownership patterns may bring certain modifications to present access arrangements.

Safety

The routes described in this guide vary considerably in both length and difficulty. Some at least of the easy walks should with reasonable care be safe at any time of the year and under almost any weather conditions; the more difficult walks on the other hand cross some of the wildest and roughest country in Great Britain and should only be attempted by fit walkers who are properly clothed and equipped and have command of the techniques involved in walking, and route finding.

It cannot be too strongly emphasized that weather and conditions can change very rapidly in moorland areas, during a day, from one part of the moorland to another or as you climb to higher ground. Hot summer days are frequent and have their hazards—sunburn, heat exhaustion and heat strokes can occur unless walkers are properly prepared. This must be borne in mind when selecting clothing and equipment before a walk. The severity of a walk will also generally be much greater in the winter.

The golden rules for safety in moorland and mountain areas are:

DO
Carry appropriate clothing and equipment, all of which should be in sound condition.
Carry map and compass; be practised in their use.
Leave a note of your intended route with a responsible person (and keep to it!).
Report your return as soon as possible.
Keep warm, but not overwarm, at all times.
Eat nourishing foods and rest at regular intervals.
Avoid becoming exhausted.
Know First Aid and the correct procedure in case of accidents or illness.
Obtain a weather forecast before you start.
For Dartmoor, you can telephone for recorded Weather Forecasts, based on Meteorological Office information, on Exeter (0392) 8091, Torquay (0803) 8091 or Plymouth (0752) 8091.

DO NOT
Go out on your own unless you are very experienced; three is a good number.
Leave any member of the party behind on remote moorland, unless help has to be summoned.
Explore old mine workings or caves, or climb cliffs (except scrambling ridges).
Attempt routes which are beyond your skill and experience.

A booklet, *Safety on Mountains,* is published by the British Mountaineering Council, Crawford House, Precinct Centre, Booth Street East, Manchester M13 9RZ.

Giving a Grid Reference

Giving a grid reference is an excellent way of 'pinpointing' a feature, such as a church or tor on an Ordnance Survey map.

Grid lines, which are used for this purpose, are shown on the 1:25 000 Outdoor Leisure, 1:25 000 Pathfinder and 1:50 000 Landranger maps produced by the Ordnance Survey; these are the maps most commonly used by walkers. They are the thin blue lines (one kilometre apart) going vertically and horizontally across the map producing a network of small squares. Each line, whether vertical or horizontal, is given a number from 00 to 99, with the sequence repeating itself every 100 lines. The 00 lines are slightly thicker than the others thus producing large squares with sides made up of 100 small squares and thus representing 100 kilometres. Each of these large squares is identified by two letters. The entire network of lines covering the British Isles, excluding Ireland, is called the National Grid.

FIGURE 3 Giving a
grid reference

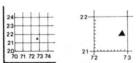

This shows a corner of an Ordnance Survey 1:50 000 Landranger map which contains a Youth Hostel. Using this map, the method of determining a grid reference is as follows:

Step 1
Holding the map in the normal upright position, note the number of the 'vertical' grid line to the left of the hostel. This is 72.

Step 2
Now imagine that the space between this grid line and the adjacent one to the right of the hostel is divided into ten equal divisions (the diagram on the right does this for you). Estimate the number of these 'tenths' that the hostel lies to the right of the left-hand grid line. This is 8. Add this to the number found in Step 1 to make 728.

Step 3
Note the number of the grid line below the hostel and add it on to the number obtained above. This is 21, so that the number becomes 72821.

Step 4
Repeat Step 2 for the space containing the hostel, but now in a vertical direction. The final number to be added is 5, making 728215. This is called a six-figure grid reference. This, coupled with the number or name of the appropriate Landranger or Outdoor Leisure map, will enable the Youth Hostel to be found.

A full grid reference will also include the identification of the appropriate 100 kilometre square of the National Grid; for example, SD 728215. This information is given in the margin of each map.

Countryside Access Charter

YOUR RIGHTS OF WAY ARE

Public footpaths—on foot only. Sometimes waymarked in yellow

Bridleways—on foot, horseback and pedal cycle. Sometimes waymarked in blue

Byways (usually old roads), most 'Roads Used as Public Paths' and, of course, public roads—all traffic.

Use maps, signs and waymarks. Ordnance Survey Pathfinder and Landranger maps show most public rights of way.

ON RIGHTS OF WAY YOU CAN

Take a pram, pushchair or wheelchair if practicable

Take a dog (on a lead or under close control)

Take a short route round an illegal obstruction or remove it sufficiently to get past.

YOU HAVE A RIGHT TO GO FOR RECREATION TO

Public parks and open spaces—on foot

Most commons near older towns and cities—on foot and sometimes on horseback

Private land where the owner has a formal agreement with the local authority.

IN ADDITION YOU CAN USE BY LOCAL OR ESTABLISHED CUSTOM OR CONSENT, BUT ASK FOR ADVICE IF YOU'RE UNSURE

Many areas of open country like moorland, fell and coastal areas, especially those of the National Trust and some commons

Some woods and forests, especially those owned by the Forestry Commission

Country Parks and picnic sites

Most beaches

Canal towpaths

Some private paths and tracks. Consent sometimes extends to riding horses and pedal cycles.

FOR YOUR INFORMATION

County councils and London boroughs maintain and record rights of way, and register commons

Obstruction, dangerous animals, harassment and misleading signs on rights of way are illegal and you should report them to the county council

Paths across fields can be ploughed, but must normally be reinstated within two weeks

Landowners can require you to leave land to which you have no right of access

Motor vehicles are normally permitted only on roads, byways and some 'Roads Used as Public Paths'

Follow any local byelaws.

AND, WHEREVER YOU GO, FOLLOW THE COUNTRY CODE

Enjoy the countryside and respect its life and work

Guard against all risk of fire

Fasten all gates

Keep your dogs under close control

Keep to public paths across farmland

Use gates and stiles to cross fences, hedges and walls

Leave livestock, crops and machinery alone

Take your litter home

Help to keep all water clean

Protect wildlife, plants and trees

Take special care on country roads

Make no unnecessary noise.

This Charter is for practical guidance in England and Wales only.

Addresses of Useful Organizations

British Trust for Conservation Volunteers
36 St Mary's Street
Wallingford
Oxfordshire
Wallingford (0491) 39766

The Camping and Caravanning Club
of Great Britain and Ireland Ltd
11 Lower Grosvenor Place
London, SW1W 0EY
01-828 1012

Council for National Parks
45 Shelton Street
London, WC2H 9HJ
01-240 3603

Countryside Commission
John Dower House
Crescent Place
Cheltenham
Gloucestershire, GL50 3RA
Cheltenham (0242) 521381

(Countryside Commission regional office)
South West Regional Office
Bridge House
Sion Place
Clifton Down
Bristol, BS8 4AS
Bristol (0272) 739966

Dartmoor National Park Authority
Parke
Haytor Road
Bovey Tracey, TQ13 9JQ
Bovey Tracey (0626) 832093

Dartmoor Preservation Association
Secretary
Crossings Cottage
Dousland
Yelverton
Plymouth, PL20 6LU

Devon Trust for Nature Conservation
35 New Bridge Street
Exeter, EX4 3AH
Exeter (0392) 79244

Exmoor National Park Authority
Exmoor House
Dulverton
Somerset, TA22 9HL
Dulverton (0398) 23665

The Exmoor Society
Parish Rooms
Dulverton
Somerset, TA22 9DP
Dulverton (0398) 23335

The National Trust
Devon Regional Office
Killerton House
Broadclyst
Exeter, EX5 3LE
Exeter (0392) 881691

The National Trust
Wessex Regional Office
Stourton
Warminster
Wiltshire, BA12 6QD
Bourton (0747) 840224

South West Water
Peninsula House
Rydon Lane
Exeter, EX2 7HR
Exeter (0392) 219666

Nature Conservancy Council
Northminster House
Northminster Road
Peterborough
Cambridgeshire, PE1 1UA
Peterborough (0733) 40345

(Regional Office)
Roughmoor
Bishop's Mull
Taunton
Somerset

West Country Tourist Board
Trinity Court
Southernhay East
Exeter, EX1 1QS
Exeter (0392) 76351

INDEX

Place names only are included. Page numbers in *italics* refer to illustrations.